Mometrix
TEST PREPARATION

I0866885

Florida

Grade 4 Mathematics Test Prep Guide

DEAR FUTURE EXAM SUCCESS STORY

First of all, **THANK YOU** for purchasing Mometrix study materials!

Second, congratulations! You are one of the few determined test-takers who are committed to doing whatever it takes to excel on your exam. **You have come to the right place.** We developed these study materials with one goal in mind: to deliver you the information you need in a format that's concise and easy to use.

In addition to optimizing your guide for the content of the test, we've outlined our recommended steps for breaking down the preparation process into small, attainable goals so you can make sure you stay on track.

We've also analyzed the entire test-taking process, identifying the most common pitfalls and showing how you can overcome them and be ready for any curveball the test throws you.

Standardized testing is one of the biggest obstacles on your road to success, which only increases the importance of doing well in the high-pressure, high-stakes environment of test day. Your results on this test could have a significant impact on your future, and this guide provides the information and practical advice to help you achieve your full potential on test day.

Your success is our success

We would love to hear from you! If you would like to share the story of your exam success or if you have any questions or comments in regard to our products, please contact us at **800-673-8175** or **support@mometrix.com**.

Thanks again for your business and we wish you continued success!

Sincerely,
The Mometrix Test Preparation Team

Written and edited by the Mometrix Exam Secrets Test Prep Team
Printed in the United States of America

TABLE OF CONTENTS

INTRODUCTION 1

SECRET KEY #1 – PLAN BIG, STUDY SMALL 2

SECRET KEY #2 – MAKE YOUR STUDYING COUNT 3

SECRET KEY #3 – PRACTICE THE RIGHT WAY 4

SECRET KEY #4 – PACE YOURSELF 6

SECRET KEY #5 – HAVE A PLAN FOR GUESSING 7

TEST-TAKING STRATEGIES 10

NUMBER SENSE AND OPERATIONS WITH WHOLE NUMBERS 15

- BASE-TEN NUMBER SYSTEM 15
- PLACE VALUE 15
- EXPANDED NOTATION 16
- WHOLE NUMBERS 17
- REPRESENTING MULTIPLICATION 18
- RECALLING MULTIPLICATION FACTS 18
- STRATEGIES FOR MULTIPLICATION 19
- MULTIPLYING BY 10 AND 100 20
- QUOTIENTS 21
- FINDING UNKNOWN NUMBERS 21
- PRIME AND COMPOSITE NUMBERS 22
- MULTIPLICATION WITH MULTIPLE-DIGIT NUMBERS 22
- DIVISION WITH MULTIPLE-DIGIT NUMBERS 24
- ESTIMATING SOLUTIONS 25
- SOLVING PROBLEMS 27
- INPUT-OUTPUT TABLES 29

NUMBER SENSE AND OPERATIONS WITH FRACTIONS AND DECIMALS 31

- DECIMALS 31
- FRACTIONS 37
- DECIMALS AND FRACTIONS ON A NUMBER LINE 46

GEOMETRIC REASONING, MEASUREMENT, AND DATA ANALYSIS AND PROBABILITY 47

- GEOMETRY TERMS 47
- RIGHT, ACUTE, AND OBTUSE ANGLES 48
- MEASURING ANGLES 49
- SOLVING FOR UNKNOWN ANGLE MEASUREMENTS 51
- RELATIVE SIZES OF MEASUREMENTS 52
- CONVERTING BETWEEN UNITS 53
- SOLVING PROBLEMS INVOLVING MEASUREMENTS 54
- SOLVING USING THE AREA AND PERIMETER OF RECTANGLES 55
- REPRESENTING DATA 57
- COMPARING DATA 60
- TIME 64

TIME INTERVALS ____ 65
PRACTICE TEST #1 ____ 66
ANSWERS AND EXPLANATIONS FOR TEST #1 ____ 78
PRACTICE TEST #2 ____ 83
ANSWERS AND EXPLANATIONS FOR TEST #2 ____ 93
HOW TO OVERCOME TEST ANXIETY ____ 97
ONLINE RESOURCES ____ 103

Introduction

Thank you for purchasing this resource! You have made the choice to prepare yourself for a test that could have a huge impact on your future, and this guide is designed to help you be fully ready for test day. Obviously, it's important to have a solid understanding of the test material, but you also need to be prepared for the unique environment and stressors of the test, so that you can perform to the best of your abilities.

For this purpose, the first section that appears in this guide is the **Secret Keys**. We've devoted countless hours to meticulously researching what works and what doesn't, and we've boiled down our findings to the five most impactful steps you can take to improve your performance on the test. We start at the beginning with study planning and move through the preparation process, all the way to the testing strategies that will help you get the most out of what you know when you're finally sitting in front of the test.

We recommend that you start preparing for your test as far in advance as possible. However, if you've bought this guide as a last-minute study resource and only have a few days before your test, we recommend that you skip over the first two Secret Keys since they address a long-term study plan.

If you struggle with **test anxiety**, we strongly encourage you to check out our recommendations for how you can overcome it. Test anxiety is a formidable foe, but it can be beaten, and we want to make sure you have the tools you need to defeat it.

Secret Key #1 – Plan Big, Study Small

There's a lot riding on your performance. If you want to ace this test, you're going to need to keep your skills sharp and the material fresh in your mind. You need a plan that lets you review everything you need to know while still fitting in your schedule. We'll break this strategy down into three categories.

Information Organization

Start with the information you already have: the official test outline. From this, you can make a complete list of all the concepts you need to cover before the test. Organize these concepts into groups that can be studied together, and create a list of any related vocabulary you need to learn so you can brush up on any difficult terms. You'll want to keep this vocabulary list handy once you actually start studying since you may need to add to it along the way.

Time Management

Once you have your set of study concepts, decide how to spread them out over the time you have left before the test. Break your study plan into small, clear goals so you have a manageable task for each day and know exactly what you're doing. Then just focus on one small step at a time. When you manage your time this way, you don't need to spend hours at a time studying. Studying a small block of content for a short period each day helps you retain information better and avoid stressing over how much you have left to do. You can relax knowing that you have a plan to cover everything in time. In order for this strategy to be effective though, you have to start studying early and stick to your schedule. Avoid the exhaustion and futility that comes from last-minute cramming!

Study Environment

The environment you study in has a big impact on your learning. Studying in a coffee shop, while probably more enjoyable, is not likely to be as fruitful as studying in a quiet room. It's important to keep distractions to a minimum. You're only planning to study for a short block of time, so make the most of it. Don't pause to check your phone or get up to find a snack. It's also important to **avoid multitasking**. Research has consistently shown that multitasking will make your studying dramatically less effective. Your study area should also be comfortable and well-lit so you don't have the distraction of straining your eyes or sitting on an uncomfortable chair.

The time of day you study is also important. You want to be rested and alert. Don't wait until just before bedtime. Study when you'll be most likely to comprehend and remember. Even better, if you know what time of day your test will be, set that time aside for study. That way your brain will be used to working on that subject at that specific time and you'll have a better chance of recalling information.

Finally, it can be helpful to team up with others who are studying for the same test. Your actual studying should be done in as isolated an environment as possible, but the work of organizing the information and setting up the study plan can be divided up. In between study sessions, you can discuss with your teammates the concepts that you're all studying and quiz each other on the details. Just be sure that your teammates are as serious about the test as you are. If you find that your study time is being replaced with social time, you might need to find a new team.

Secret Key #2 – Make Your Studying Count

You're devoting a lot of time and effort to preparing for this test, so you want to be absolutely certain it will pay off. This means doing more than just reading the content and hoping you can remember it on test day. It's important to make every minute of study count. There are two main areas you can focus on to make your studying count.

Retention

It doesn't matter how much time you study if you can't remember the material. You need to make sure you are retaining the concepts. To check your retention of the information you're learning, try recalling it at later times with minimal prompting. Try carrying around flashcards and glance at one or two from time to time or ask a friend who's also studying for the test to quiz you.

To enhance your retention, look for ways to put the information into practice so that you can apply it rather than simply recalling it. If you're using the information in practical ways, it will be much easier to remember. Similarly, it helps to solidify a concept in your mind if you're not only reading it to yourself but also explaining it to someone else. Ask a friend to let you teach them about a concept you're a little shaky on (or speak aloud to an imaginary audience if necessary). As you try to summarize, define, give examples, and answer your friend's questions, you'll understand the concepts better and they will stay with you longer. Finally, step back for a big picture view and ask yourself how each piece of information fits with the whole subject. When you link the different concepts together and see them working together as a whole, it's easier to remember the individual components.

Finally, practice showing your work on any multi-step problems, even if you're just studying. Writing out each step you take to solve a problem will help solidify the process in your mind, and you'll be more likely to remember it during the test.

Modality

Modality simply refers to the means or method by which you study. Choosing a study modality that fits your own individual learning style is crucial. No two people learn best in exactly the same way, so it's important to know your strengths and use them to your advantage.

For example, if you learn best by visualization, focus on visualizing a concept in your mind and draw an image or a diagram. Try color-coding your notes, illustrating them, or creating symbols that will trigger your mind to recall a learned concept. If you learn best by hearing or discussing information, find a study partner who learns the same way or read aloud to yourself. Think about how to put the information in your own words. Imagine that you are giving a lecture on the topic and record yourself so you can listen to it later.

For any learning style, flashcards can be helpful. Organize the information so you can take advantage of spare moments to review. Underline key words or phrases. Use different colors for different categories. Mnemonic devices (such as creating a short list in which every item starts with the same letter) can also help with retention. Find what works best for you and use it to store the information in your mind most effectively and easily.

Secret Key #3 – Practice the Right Way

Your success on test day depends not only on how many hours you put into preparing, but also on whether you prepared the right way. It's good to check along the way to see if your studying is paying off. One of the most effective ways to do this is by taking practice tests to evaluate your progress. Practice tests are useful because they show exactly where you need to improve. Every time you take a practice test, pay special attention to these three groups of questions:

- The questions you got wrong
- The questions you had to guess on, even if you guessed right
- The questions you found difficult or slow to work through

This will show you exactly what your weak areas are, and where you need to devote more study time. Ask yourself why each of these questions gave you trouble. Was it because you didn't understand the material? Was it because you didn't remember the vocabulary? Do you need more repetitions on this type of question to build speed and confidence? Dig into those questions and figure out how you can strengthen your weak areas as you go back to review the material.

Additionally, many practice tests have a section explaining the answer choices. It can be tempting to read the explanation and think that you now have a good understanding of the concept. However, an explanation likely only covers part of the question's broader context. Even if the explanation makes perfect sense, **go back and investigate** every concept related to the question until you're positive you have a thorough understanding.

As you go along, keep in mind that the practice test is just that: practice. Memorizing these questions and answers will not be very helpful on the actual test because it is unlikely to have any of the same exact questions. If you only know the right answers to the sample questions, you won't be prepared for the real thing. **Study the concepts** until you understand them fully, and then you'll be able to answer any question that shows up on the test.

It's important to wait on the practice tests until you're ready. If you take a test on your first day of study, you may be overwhelmed by the amount of material covered and how much you need to learn. Work up to it gradually.

On test day, you'll need to be prepared for answering questions, managing your time, and using the test-taking strategies you've learned. It's a lot to balance, like a mental marathon that will have a big impact on your future. Like training for a marathon, you'll need to start slowly and work your way up. When test day arrives, you'll be ready.

Start with the strategies you've read in the first two Secret Keys—plan your course and study in the way that works best for you. If you have time, consider using multiple study resources to get different approaches to the same concepts. It can be helpful to see difficult concepts from more than one angle. Then find a good source for practice tests. Many times, the test website will suggest potential study resources or provide sample tests.

Practice Test Strategy

If you're able to find at least three practice tests, we recommend this strategy:

Untimed and Open-Book Practice

Take the first test with no time constraints and with your notes and study guide handy. Take your time and focus on applying the strategies you've learned.

Timed and Open-Book Practice

Take the second practice test open-book as well, but set a timer and practice pacing yourself to finish in time.

Timed and Closed-Book Practice

Take any other practice tests as if it were test day. Set a timer and put away your study materials. Sit at a table or desk in a quiet room, imagine yourself at the testing center, and answer questions as quickly and accurately as possible.

Keep repeating timed and closed-book tests on a regular basis until you run out of practice tests or it's time for the actual test. Your mind will be ready for the schedule and stress of test day, and you'll be able to focus on recalling the material you've learned.

Secret Key #4 – Pace Yourself

Once you're fully prepared for the material on the test, your biggest challenge on test day will be managing your time. Just knowing that the clock is ticking can make you panic even if you have plenty of time left. Work on pacing yourself so you can build confidence against the time constraints of the exam. Pacing is a difficult skill to master, especially in a high-pressure environment, so **practice is vital**.

Set time expectations for your pace based on how much time is available. For example, if a section has 60 questions and the time limit is 30 minutes, you know you have to average 30 seconds or less per question in order to answer them all. Although 30 seconds is the hard limit, set 25 seconds per question as your goal, so you reserve extra time to spend on harder questions. When you budget extra time for the harder questions, you no longer have any reason to stress when those questions take longer to answer.

Don't let this time expectation distract you from working through the test at a calm, steady pace, but keep it in mind so you don't spend too much time on any one question. Recognize that taking extra time on one question you don't understand may keep you from answering two that you do understand later in the test. If your time limit for a question is up and you're still not sure of the answer, mark it and move on, and come back to it later if the time and the test format allow. If the testing format doesn't allow you to return to earlier questions, just make an educated guess; then put it out of your mind and move on.

On the easier questions, be careful not to rush. It may seem wise to hurry through them so you have more time for the challenging ones, but it's not worth missing one if you know the concept and just didn't take the time to read the question fully. Work efficiently but make sure you understand the question and have looked at all of the answer choices, since more than one may seem right at first.

Even if you're paying attention to the time, you may find yourself a little behind at some point. You should speed up to get back on track, but do so wisely. Don't panic; just take a few seconds less on each question until you're caught up. Don't guess without thinking, but do look through the answer choices and eliminate any you know are wrong. If you can get down to two choices, it is often worthwhile to guess from those. Once you've chosen an answer, move on and don't dwell on any that you skipped or had to hurry through. If a question was taking too long, chances are it was one of the harder ones, so you weren't as likely to get it right anyway.

On the other hand, if you find yourself getting ahead of schedule, it may be beneficial to slow down a little. The more quickly you work, the more likely you are to make a careless mistake that will affect your score. You've budgeted time for each question, so don't be afraid to spend that time. Practice an efficient but careful pace to get the most out of the time you have.

Secret Key #5 – Have a Plan for Guessing

When you're taking the test, you may find yourself stuck on a question. Some of the answer choices seem better than others, but you don't see the one answer choice that is obviously correct. What do you do?

The scenario described above is very common, yet most test takers have not effectively prepared for it. Developing and practicing a plan for guessing may be one of the single most effective uses of your time as you get ready for the exam.

In developing your plan for guessing, there are three questions to address:

- When should you start the guessing process?
- How should you narrow down the choices?
- Which answer should you choose?

When to Start the Guessing Process

Unless your plan for guessing is to select C every time (which, despite its merits, is not what we recommend), you need to leave yourself enough time to apply your answer elimination strategies. Since you have a limited amount of time for each question, that means that if you're going to give yourself the best shot at guessing correctly, you have to decide quickly whether or not you will guess.

Of course, the best-case scenario is that you don't have to guess at all, so first, see if you can answer the question based on your knowledge of the subject and basic reasoning skills. Focus on the key words in the question and try to jog your memory of related topics. Give yourself a chance to bring the knowledge to mind, but once you realize that you don't have (or you can't access) the knowledge you need to answer the question, it's time to start the guessing process.

It's almost always better to start the guessing process too early than too late. It only takes a few seconds to remember something and answer the question from knowledge. Carefully eliminating wrong answer choices takes longer. Plus, going through the process of eliminating answer choices can actually help jog your memory.

Summary: Start the guessing process as soon as you decide that you can't answer the question based on your knowledge.

How to Narrow Down the Choices

The next chapter in this book (**Test-Taking Strategies**) includes a wide range of strategies for how to approach questions and how to look for answer choices to eliminate. You will definitely want to read those carefully, practice them, and figure out which ones work best for you. Here though, we're going to address a mindset rather than a particular strategy.

Your odds of guessing an answer correctly depend on how many options you are choosing from.

Number of options left	5	4	3	2	1
Odds of guessing correctly	20%	25%	33%	50%	100%

You can see from this chart just how valuable it is to be able to eliminate incorrect answers and make an educated guess, but there are two things that many test takers do that cause them to miss out on the benefits of guessing:

- Accidentally eliminating the correct answer
- Selecting an answer based on an impression

We'll look at the first one here, and the second one in the next section.

To avoid accidentally eliminating the correct answer, we recommend a thought exercise called **the $5 challenge**. In this challenge, you only eliminate an answer choice from contention if you are willing to bet $5 on it being wrong. Why $5? Five dollars is a small but not insignificant amount of money. It's an amount you could afford to lose but wouldn't want to throw away. And while losing $5 once might not hurt too much, doing it twenty times will set you back $100. In the same way, each small decision you make—eliminating a choice here, guessing on a question there—won't by itself impact your score very much, but when you put them all together, they can make a big difference. By holding each answer choice elimination decision to a higher standard, you can reduce the risk of accidentally eliminating the correct answer.

The $5 challenge can also be applied in a positive sense: If you are willing to bet $5 that an answer choice *is* correct, go ahead and mark it as correct.

Summary: Only eliminate an answer choice if you are willing to bet $5 that it is wrong.

Which Answer to Choose

You're taking the test. You've run into a hard question and decided you'll have to guess. You've eliminated all the answer choices you're willing to bet $5 on. Now you have to pick an answer. Why do we even need to talk about this? Why can't you just pick whichever one you feel like when the time comes?

The answer to these questions is that if you don't come into the test with a plan, you'll rely on your impression to select an answer choice, and if you do that, you risk falling into a trap. The test writers know that everyone who takes their test will be guessing on some of the questions, so they intentionally write wrong answer choices to seem plausible. You still have to pick an answer though, and if the wrong answer choices are designed to look right, how can you ever be sure that you're not falling for their trap? The best solution we've found to this dilemma is to take the decision out of your hands entirely. Here is the process we recommend:

Once you've eliminated any choices that you are confident (willing to bet $5) are wrong, select the first remaining choice as your answer.

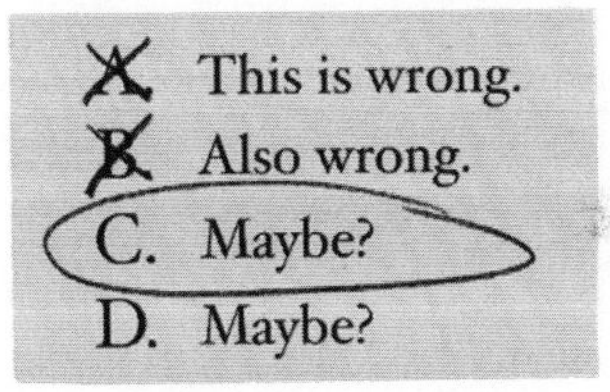

Whether you choose to select the first remaining choice, the second, or the last, the important thing is that you use some preselected standard. Using this approach guarantees that you will not be enticed into selecting an answer choice that looks right, because you are not basing your decision on how the answer choices look.

This is not meant to make you question your knowledge. Instead, it is to help you recognize the difference between your knowledge and your impressions. There's a huge difference between thinking an answer is right because of what you know, and thinking an answer is right because it looks or sounds like it should be right.

Summary: To ensure that your selection is appropriately random, make a predetermined selection from among all answer choices you have not eliminated.

Test-Taking Strategies

This section contains a list of test-taking strategies that you may find helpful as you work through the test. By taking what you know and applying logical thought, you can maximize your chances of answering any question correctly!

It is very important to realize that every question is different and every person is different: no single strategy will work on every question, and no single strategy will work for every person. That's why we've included all of them here, so you can try them out and determine which ones work best for different types of questions and which ones work best for you.

Question Strategies

✓ Read Carefully

Read the question and the answer choices carefully. Don't miss the question because you misread the terms. You have plenty of time to read each question thoroughly and make sure you understand what is being asked. Yet a happy medium must be attained, so don't waste too much time. You must read carefully and efficiently.

✓ Contextual Clues

Look for contextual clues. If the question includes a word you are not familiar with, look at the immediate context for some indication of what the word might mean. Contextual clues can often give you all the information you need to decipher the meaning of an unfamiliar word. Even if you can't determine the meaning, you may be able to narrow down the possibilities enough to make a solid guess at the answer to the question.

✓ Prefixes

If you're having trouble with a word in the question or answer choices, try dissecting it. Take advantage of every clue that the word might include. Prefixes can be a huge help. Usually, they allow you to determine a basic meaning. *Pre-* means before, *post-* means after, *pro-* is positive, *de-* is negative. From prefixes, you can get an idea of the general meaning of the word and try to put it into context.

✓ Hedge Words

Watch out for critical hedge words, such as *likely, may, can, often, almost, mostly, usually, generally, rarely,* and *sometimes.* Question writers insert these hedge phrases to cover every possibility. Often an answer choice will be wrong simply because it leaves no room for exception. Be on guard for answer choices that have definitive words such as *exactly* and *always.*

✓ Switchback Words

Stay alert for *switchbacks.* These are the words and phrases frequently used to alert you to shifts in thought. The most common switchback words are *but, although,* and *however.* Others include *nevertheless, on the other hand, even though, while, in spite of, despite,* and *regardless of.* Switchback words are important to catch because they can change the direction of the question or an answer choice.

☑ FACE VALUE

When in doubt, use common sense. Accept the situation in the problem at face value. Don't read too much into it. These problems will not require you to make wild assumptions. If you have to go beyond creativity and warp time or space in order to have an answer choice fit the question, then you should move on and consider the other answer choices. These are normal problems rooted in reality. The applicable relationship or explanation may not be readily apparent, but it is there for you to figure out. Use your common sense to interpret anything that isn't clear.

Answer Choice Strategies

☑ ANSWER SELECTION

The most thorough way to pick an answer choice is to identify and eliminate wrong answers until only one is left, then confirm it is the correct answer. Sometimes an answer choice may immediately seem right, but be careful. The test writers will usually put more than one reasonable answer choice on each question, so take a second to read all of them and make sure that the other choices are not equally obvious. As long as you have time left, it is better to read every answer choice than to pick the first one that looks right without checking the others.

☑ ANSWER CHOICE FAMILIES

An answer choice family consists of two (in rare cases, three) answer choices that are very similar in construction and cannot all be true at the same time. If you see two answer choices that are direct opposites or parallels, one of them is usually the correct answer. For instance, if one answer choice says that quantity *x* increases and another either says that quantity *x* decreases (opposite) or says that quantity *y* increases (parallel), then those answer choices would fall into the same family. An answer choice that doesn't match the construction of the answer choice family is more likely to be incorrect. Most questions will not have answer choice families, but when they do appear, you should be prepared to recognize them.

☑ ELIMINATE ANSWERS

Eliminate answer choices as soon as you realize they are wrong, but make sure you consider all possibilities. If you are eliminating answer choices and realize that the last one you are left with is also wrong, don't panic. Start over and consider each choice again. There may be something you missed the first time that you will realize on the second pass.

☑ AVOID FACT TRAPS

Don't be distracted by an answer choice that is factually true but doesn't answer the question. You are looking for the choice that answers the question. Stay focused on what the question is asking for so you don't accidentally pick an answer that is true but incorrect. Always go back to the question and make sure the answer choice you've selected actually answers the question and is not merely a true statement.

☑ EXTREME STATEMENTS

In general, you should avoid answers that put forth extreme actions as standard practice or proclaim controversial ideas as established fact. An answer choice that states the "process should be used in certain situations, if..." is much more likely to be correct than one that states the "process should be discontinued completely." The first is a calm rational statement and doesn't even make a definitive, uncompromising stance, using a hedge word *if* to provide wiggle room, whereas the second choice is far more extreme.

⊘ BENCHMARK

As you read through the answer choices and you come across one that seems to answer the question well, mentally select that answer choice. This is not your final answer, but it's the one that will help you evaluate the other answer choices. The one that you selected is your benchmark or standard for judging each of the other answer choices. Every other answer choice must be compared to your benchmark. That choice is correct until proven otherwise by another answer choice beating it. If you find a better answer, then that one becomes your new benchmark. Once you've decided that no other choice answers the question as well as your benchmark, you have your final answer.

⊘ PREDICT THE ANSWER

Before you even start looking at the answer choices, it is often best to try to predict the answer. When you come up with the answer on your own, it is easier to avoid distractions and traps because you will know exactly what to look for. The right answer choice is unlikely to be word-for-word what you came up with, but it should be a close match. Even if you are confident that you have the right answer, you should still take the time to read each option before moving on.

General Strategies

⊘ TOUGH QUESTIONS

If you are stumped on a problem or it appears too hard or too difficult, don't waste time. Move on! Remember though, if you can quickly check for obviously incorrect answer choices, your chances of guessing correctly are greatly improved. Before you completely give up, at least try to knock out a couple of possible answers. Eliminate what you can and then guess at the remaining answer choices before moving on.

⊘ CHECK YOUR WORK

Since you will probably not know every term listed and the answer to every question, it is important that you get credit for the ones that you do know. Don't miss any questions through careless mistakes. If at all possible, try to take a second to look back over your answer selection and make sure you've selected the correct answer choice and haven't made a costly careless mistake (such as marking an answer choice that you didn't mean to mark). This quick double check should more than pay for itself in caught mistakes for the time it costs.

⊘ PACE YOURSELF

It's easy to be overwhelmed when you're looking at a page full of questions; your mind is confused and full of random thoughts, and the clock is ticking down faster than you would like. Calm down and maintain the pace that you have set for yourself. Especially as you get down to the last few minutes of the test, don't let the small numbers on the clock make you panic. As long as you are on track by monitoring your pace, you are guaranteed to have time for each question.

⊘ DON'T RUSH

It is very easy to make errors when you are in a hurry. Maintaining a fast pace in answering questions is pointless if it makes you miss questions that you would have gotten right otherwise. Test writers like to include distracting information and wrong answers that seem right. Taking a little extra time to avoid careless mistakes can make all the difference in your test score. Find a pace that allows you to be confident in the answers that you select.

⊘ Keep Moving

Panicking will not help you pass the test, so do your best to stay calm and keep moving. Taking deep breaths and going through the answer elimination steps you practiced can help to break through a stress barrier and keep your pace.

Final Notes

The combination of a solid foundation of content knowledge and the confidence that comes from practicing your plan for applying that knowledge is the key to maximizing your performance on test day. As your foundation of content knowledge is built up and strengthened, you'll find that the strategies included in this chapter become more and more effective in helping you quickly sift through the distractions and traps of the test to isolate the correct answer.

Now that you're preparing to move forward into the test content chapters of this book, be sure to keep your goal in mind. As you read, think about how you will be able to apply this information on the test. If you've already seen sample questions for the test and you have an idea of the question format and style, try to come up with questions of your own that you can answer based on what you're reading. This will give you valuable practice applying your knowledge in the same ways you can expect to on test day.

Good luck and good studying!

Number Sense and Operations with Whole Numbers

Base-Ten Number System

In the **base ten number system**, digits **increase** by a **factor of 10** as you move to the **left** and **decrease** by a factor of 10 as you move to the **right**. For example, 55.55 shows 5 in the hundredths place, 5 in the tenths place, 5 in the ones place, and 5 in the tens place. Digits are 10 times as large as you move to the left. As you move to the right, the digits are one-tenth the previous digit.

Moving to the left:

$\frac{5}{10}$ is 10 times as large as $\frac{5}{100}$.

5 is 10 times as large as $\frac{5}{10}$.

50 is 10 times as large as 5.

Moving to the right:

5 is $\frac{1}{10}$ of 50.

0.5 is $\frac{1}{10}$ of 5.

0.05 is $\frac{1}{10}$ of 0.5.

Place Value

Numbers can be broken apart and composed based on their **place value**. For example, the number 129,548 can be expressed in **expanded form** as 100,000 + 20,000 + 9,000 + 500 + 40 + 8. You should also be comfortable going from expanded form to standard form. For example, what number is represented by 30,000 + 400 + 80 + 2? Notice 3 groups of ten-thousands, 0 groups of thousands, 4 groups of hundreds, 8 groups of tens, and 2 groups of ones. This becomes 30,482.

Sometimes you will be asked to compose and decompose numbers that are presented in **picture** or **model** form. This usually includes base-10 blocks. For example, consider the model below. How many groups of thousands, hundreds, tens, and ones are there? There is 1 group of 1,000, 2 groups of 100, 4 groups of 10, and 7 ones. This forms the number 1,247.

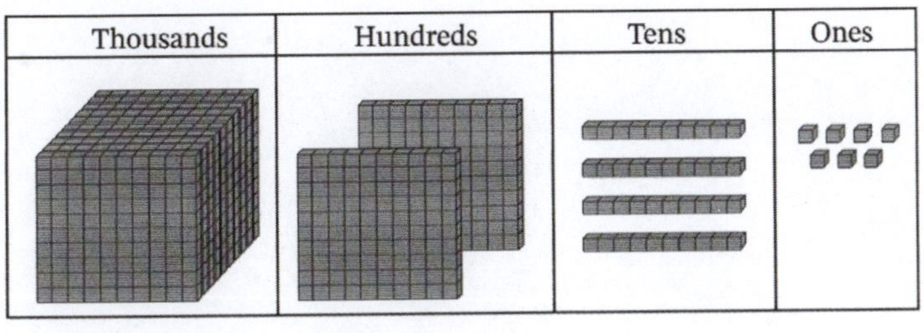

Expanded Notation

Expanded notation shows the value of each digit in a number. For example, 45.3 can be "expanded" into 4 tens, 5 ones, and 3 tenths. In expanded form, it is $40 + 5 + 0.3$.

The following number is in **standard form**: 1,234,567,891.23

When writing numbers in expanded form, consider the place value of each number.

The first 1 represents 1,000,000,000.
The first 2 represents 200,000,000.
The first 3 represents 30,000,000.
The 4 represents 4,000,000.
The 5 represents 500,000.
The 6 represents 60,000.
The 7 represents 7,000.
The 8 represents 800.
The 9 represents 90.
The second 1 represents 1.
The second 2 represents 0.2.
The second 3 represents 0.03.

Put it all together in expanded form:

$$1{,}000{,}000{,}000 + 200{,}000{,}000 + 30{,}000{,}000 + 4{,}000{,}000 + 500{,}000 + 60{,}000 + 7{,}000 + 800 + 90 + 1 + 0.2 + 0.03$$

Review Video: Place Value
Visit mometrix.com/academy and enter code: 205433

Example

Write the number 567.92 in expanded form.

Standard form: 567.92

Expanded form: $500 + 60 + 7 + 0.9 + 0.02$

Example

What is the value of the first 5 in the number 45,105,000?

The first 5 is in the millions place, so its value is 5,000,000.

Whole Numbers

Comparing Whole Numbers

When comparing whole numbers, compare each digit from left to right. For example, consider the comparison between the numbers 46,241,733 and 46,243,946. At first glance, the numbers might seem very close. To precisely compare the numbers, compare each digit, one by one, starting at the **farthest left digit**.

$$\underline{46}\ ,\ \underline{241}\ ,733$$

$$\underline{46}\ ,\ \underline{243}\ ,946$$

Both digits have 4 in the ten millions place.
Both digits have 6 in the millions place.
Both digits have 2 in the hundred thousands place.
Both digits have 4 in the ten thousands place.

The top number has 1 in the thousands place, but the bottom number has 3 in the thousands place. $3 > 1$ so $46,243,946 > 46,241,733$.

Symbols for Comparing Numbers

Remember that the symbol > means “is **greater** than.” When using this symbol, the larger number must appear first, or to the left of the symbol. The symbol < means “is **less** than.” So when using this symbol, the smaller number must appear first, or to the left of the symbol. When using the symbol =, the equal sign, the numbers on both sides of the symbol should have the **same** value.

Rounding Whole Numbers

When rounding whole numbers, look at the number to the **right** of the digit you are **rounding**. If the number to the right is **5 or more**, the digit you are rounding rounds **up**. If the number to the right is **less than 5**, the digit you are rounding stays the **same**. All the digits to the right of the one you are rounding become **zeros**.

Round to the nearest ten: 392,537

Find the digit in the tens place (3). Look to the right. 7 is “5 or more”, so the digit 3 will round up to 4. All digits to the right of 4 become 0.

392,537 becomes 392,540.

Round to the nearest hundred: 392,537.

Find the digit in the hundreds place (5). Look to the right. 3 is “less than 5”, so the digit 5 will stay the same. All digits to the right of 5 become 0.

392,537 becomes 392,500.

Round to the nearest thousand: 392,537. Find the digit in the thousands place (2). Look to the right. 5 is “5 or more”, so the digit 2 will round up to 3. All digits to the right of the rounded 3 become 0.

392,537 becomes 393,000.

Representing Multiplication

Repeated Addition

Multiplication is the process of counting equally sized groups. 5 groups of 7 means $7 + 7 + 7 + 7 + 7$. 5 groups of 7 is 35. The process of using addition to solve multiplication problems is known as **repeated addition**. This strategy is a great choice in many scenarios.

Number Lines

A number line can be used to show repeated addition. The **number line** below shows 4 equal hops of 3. 4 hops of 3 represents 4×3, which is 12: $3 + 3 + 3 + 3 = 12$.

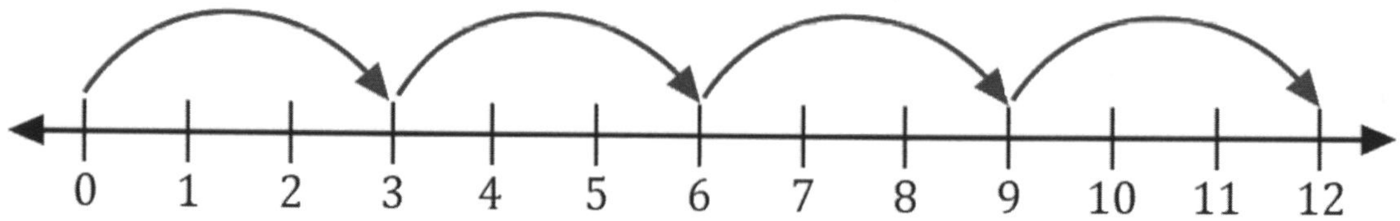

Arrays

An array is a collection and rows and columns representing a multiplication problem. This **array** has 10 columns and 4 rows. This array represents $10 \times 4 = 40$.

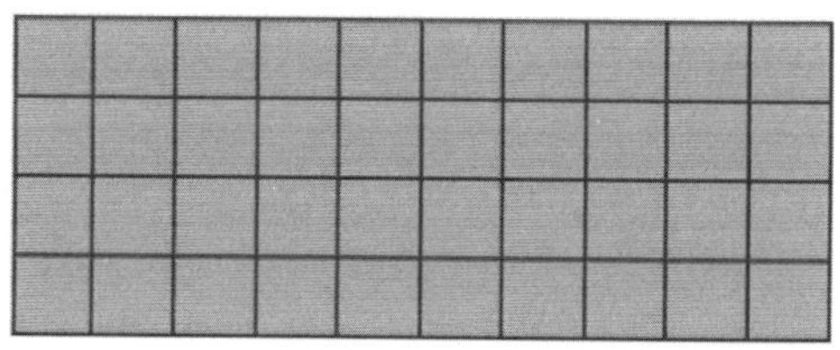

Recalling Multiplication Facts

It is a great accomplishment to memorize the multiplication and division facts from 0 to 10. This is a goal that can take some time, so keep practicing!

Some strategies that can help:

1. **Skip count by the larger number.** For example, for the problem 8×3 skip count by 8s not 3s. This can save some time. $8 + 8 + 8$ is quicker than $3 + 3 + 3 + 3 + 3 + 3 + 3 + 3$.
2. **Use facts that you do know to help you.** For example, if you are stuck on 7×4 but you know 5×7 is 35, use logic to help you. 5 groups of 7 is 7 more than 4 groups of 7, so subtract 7 from 35 to solve 4×7.
3. **Use multiplication to help with division.** Multiplication and division are inverse operations. This means they undo each other. For example, $9 \times 4 = 36$ and $4 \times 9 = 36$ represent the inverse of $36 \div 4 = 9$ and $36 \div 9 = 4$. Your multiplication facts and division facts go hand-in-hand! Remember, multiplication and division fact families use the same three numbers. For example, $8 \times 7 = 56$, $7 \times 8 = 56$, $56 \div 7 = 8$, and $56 \div 8 = 7$ all use the same three numbers.

Strategies for Multiplication

Strategies such as mental math, skip counting, and drawing a model are great for single digit multiplication problems. However, for larger numbers, these strategies are less ideal. For example, solving 7×82 by skip counting would take quite a long time. 7, 14, 21, 28... all the way up to 574! Luckily, there are faster strategies for multiplying by two-digit numbers.

Standard Algorithm

Place the two-digit number over the one-digit number. Start by multiplying the numbers in the ones place: $2 \times 7 = 14$. Regroup the 14 into 1 and 4, as shown.

Now multiply 7 by the number in the tens place: $7 \times 8 = 56$. Add the 1 from up above: $56 + 1 = 57$. Write 57 down below: $82 \times 7 = 574$.

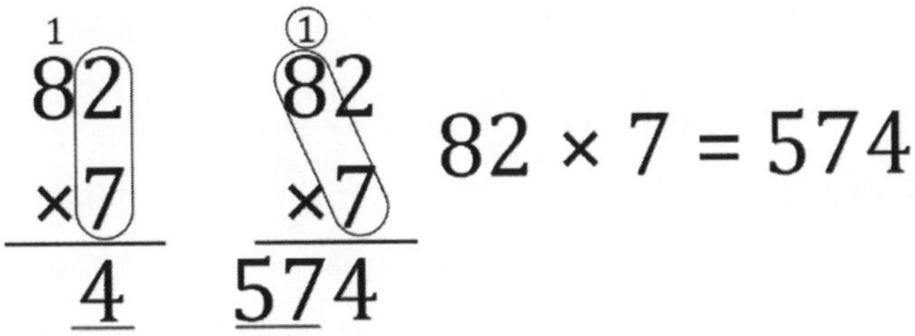

Partial Products

Think about the two-digit number in terms of its place value.

82 consists of 8 tens and 2 ones: $82 = 80 + 2$.

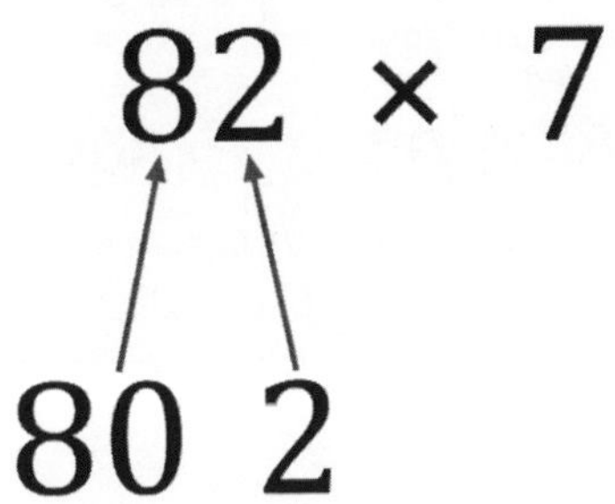

Now multiply each part by 7.

$$80 \times 7 = 560$$

$$2 \times 7 = 14$$

Now add the products.

$$\begin{array}{r} 560 \\ +\ \ 14 \\ \hline 574 \end{array}$$

$$560 + 14 = 574$$

Distributive Property

Using the **distribute property** is very similar to using **partial products**.

Distribute the 7 to each part of 82. 7 × 80 and 7 × 2.

$$7 \times 82$$

$$(7 \times 80) \quad + \quad (7 \times 2)$$

$$(7 \times 80) + (7 \times 2) = 560 + 14 = 574$$

Commutative Property

The **order** of the **factors** does not matter in multiplication.

$$3 \times 9 \times 4 = 4 \times 9 \times 3$$

Associative Property

In multiplication, the **arrangement** of **grouping symbols** does not affect the outcome.

$$(4 \times 9) \times 3 = 4 \times (9 \times 3)$$

Multiplying by 10 and 100

When multiplying by 10, the decimal point moves **one place** to the **right**. When multiplying by 100, the decimal point moves **two places** to the **right**. The pattern continues for each multiple of 10. This is a convenient way to multiply numbers by powers of 10. For example, notice the decimal movement in the following examples:

$$45.62 \times 10 = 456.2$$

$$45.62 \times 100 = 4{,}562.0$$

The same pattern can be seen when multiplying whole numbers. Any whole number can be expressed as a decimal. Think about where the decimal point is in the number 50. Sometimes the decimal point is not written for whole numbers, but it's technically there. 50 has a "decimal" to the right of the ones place. Remember, a decimal separates the ones place from the tenths place. 50 is equal to 50.0.

$$50.0 \times 10 = 500.0$$

Notice how the decimal moves one place to the right.

$$50.0 \times 100 = 5{,}000.0$$

Notice how the decimal moves two places to the right.

Quotients

Multiplication can be used to determine a **quotient**. Similar to addition and subtraction, multiplication and division are **inverse operations**. For example, $72 \div 9$ can be solved using the multiplication facts for 9. $72 \div 9 =?$ Ask the question, "9 groups of what equals 72?"

$9 \times 6 = 54 \ldots 9 \times 7 = 63 \ldots 9 \times 8 = 72$. The missing number is 8. This means $72 \div 9 = 8$. This strategy is quite helpful because once the multiplication facts are automatic, division facts become automatic as well.

Consider the following examples:

$42 \div 7 =?$ "7 groups of what equals 42?" $6 \times 7 = 42$. The product of 6 and 7 is 42. The quotient of 42 and 7 is 6.

$$42 \div 7 = 6$$

$48 \div 8 =?$ "8 groups of what equals 48?" $6 \times 8 = 48$. The product of 6 and 8 is 48. The quotient of 48 and 8 is 6.

$$48 \div 8 = 6$$

Finding Unknown Numbers

Inverse Operations

Multiplication and division go hand in hand. Division and multiplication are considered **inverse operations**, which means they are the reverse, or opposite, of each other. This can be helpful when there is an **unknown number** in an equation. For example, $4 \times ? = 24$ is a multiplication equation that can be solved using division. $24 \div 4 = 6$, therefore $4 \times 6 = 24$. The missing number is 6.

Let's try another example: $72 \div ? = 9$. This is a division equation that can be solved using multiplication. What number times 9 equals 72? The missing number is 8.

Fact Families

Don't forget to use **fact families** when solving equations with **missing numbers**.

For example, the equations $5 \times 8 = 40$, $8 \times 5 = 40$, $40 \div 5 = 8$, $40 \div 8 = 5$ represent a fact family. The same three numbers are used in all the equations. This can be helpful when one of the numbers is missing. For example, $8 \times ? = 40$. Remember the fact families. 8 groups of 5 equals 40, so the missing number is 5.

$$\text{Factor} \times \text{Factor} = \text{Product}$$

$$8 \times 5 = 40$$

8 and 5 are considered factors, and 40 is the product.

Prime and Composite Numbers

A **prime number** is a number that has exactly **2 factors**, meaning it is only divisible by 1 and itself. For example, the number 7 is prime because 7 can only be divided by 1 and 7. The first ten prime numbers are 2, 3, 5, 7, 11, 13, 17, 19, 23, and 29.

The opposite of a prime number is a composite number. **Composite numbers** have more than 2 factors, meaning they are divisible by more than 2 numbers. For example, 24 is composite because it has more than just 1 and 24 as factors. 24 consists of 1 group of 24, 2 groups of 12, 3 groups of 8, or 4 groups of 6. The factors of 24 are 1, 2, 3, 4, 6, 8, 12, and 24.

Review Video: Prime and Composite Numbers
Visit mometrix.com/academy and enter code: 565581

Multiplication with Multiple-Digit Numbers

Area Models

There are a variety of strategies to choose from when multiplying multi-digit numbers. Area models and arrays can be used to show multiplication in a visual way, as opposed to the standard algorithm. For example, consider the problem 8×11. This can be represented as an **array** with 8 columns and 11 rows. There are 8 groups of 11 stars, or 11 groups of 8 stars. The total number of stars is 88, so $8 \times 11 = 88$. This strategy is great for smaller numbers. However, when multiplying two-digit numbers an area model is often preferred.

An **area model** is a visual representation of the distributive property. For example, when multiplying 27 by 35, the distributive property would be expressed as $7 \times 5 + 7 \times 30 + 20 \times 5 + 20 \times 30$. An area model shows this process using boxes. Set up each two-digit number as shown. Break apart 27 into 20 and 7. Break apart 35 into 30 and 5. Fill in each box by multiplying the outside numbers. $30 \times 20 = 600$, $30 \times 7 = 210$, $5 \times 20 = 100$, $5 \times 7 = 35$, and the sum of all the products is $600 + 100 + 210 + 35 = 945$. Therefore, $27 \times 35 = 945$.

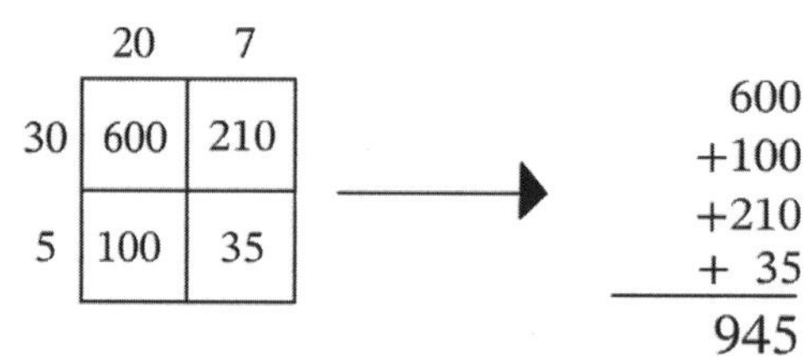

$27 \times 35 = 945$

Standard Algorithm

Area models and arrays are great strategies for one and two-digit multiplication. However, the **standard algorithm** is a commonly preferred strategy for numbers that are more than three digits. The standard algorithm, or "vertical multiplication" is less visual but more time effective. For example, consider the product $7{,}482 \times 8$. Write the longer number on the top and the shorter number on the bottom. Push all numbers to the right so that the place value is lined up (ones lined up with ones, tens lined up with tens, etc.).

$$\begin{array}{r} {\scriptstyle 3\ \ 61\ } \\ 7{,}482 \\ \times \quad\quad 8 \\ \hline 59{,}856 \end{array}$$

Distribute, or multiply, the 8 by each digit in the number 7,482. Work from right to left. 8×2, then 8×8, then 8×4, then 8×7. If a product has more than one digit, write the ones digit in the answer and carry the tens digit above the next number you are multiplying. For example, $2 \times 8 = 16$, so write 6 in the answer and 1 above 8 (the next number you will multiply by). Then, add the carried number to the next product. $8 \times 8 = 64$, then add 1 to get 65, and continue the multiplication process for the rest of the number. The product of 7,482 and 8 is 59,856.

Partial Products

Using partial products is another option when multiplying multi-digit numbers. For example, consider the problem 48×26.

Using **partial products** is one way to express the distributive property. In the problem 48×26, each digit needs to be multiplied by every other digit, according to its place value. Using partial products breaks this down into pieces.

$$6 \times 8 = 48$$
$$6 \times 40 = 240$$
$$20 \times 8 = 160$$
$$20 \times 40 = 800$$

$$\begin{array}{r} 48 \\ \times 26 \\ \hline 48 \\ 240 \\ 160 \\ +\,800 \\ \hline 1{,}248 \end{array}$$

The sum of these "partial products" is 1,248.

Division with Multiple-Digit Numbers

Area Models

Long division is not the only way to divide multi-digit numbers. You can also use an **area model**. $620 \div 5$ can be solved by drawing a rectangle with 5 as one side length. Now think in terms of multiplication. 5×100 is close to 620. Start with this. Write 100 above the rectangle. $5 \times 100 = 500$. So, write 500 in the first box.

$620 - 500 = 120$, so now think about multiplying 5 by a number to get close to 120. 5×20 is 100, so start there. Write 20 above the rectangle. Since $5 \times 20 = 100$, write 100 in the next box.

$120 - 100 = 20$, so now think about multiplying 5 by a number to get close to 20. 5×4 is 20, so write 4 above the rectangle. Write 20 in the last box.

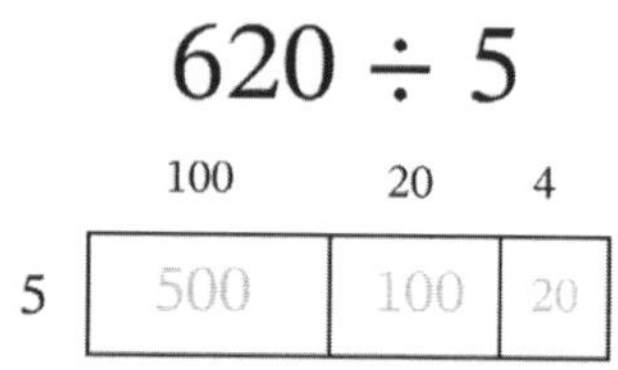

Now add up the numbers above the rectangle. $100 + 20 + 4 = 124$, therefore $620 \div 5 = 124$.

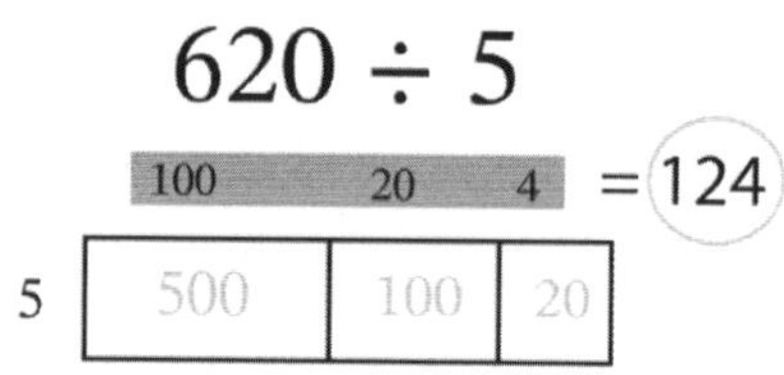

Long Division

The **standard algorithm** for division, also known as **long division**, is a great option for division problems involving large numbers. The long division process involves 4 steps that repeat in a cycle.

The divisor goes to the left of the division sign, and the dividend goes under the division sign. For example, in the problem $6{,}488 \div 2$, the divisor is 2 and the dividend is 6,488.

$$2\overline{)\,6,488}$$

The four steps of long division:

1. "How many times?"
2. Multiply
3. Subtract
4. Bring down

Example

1. 2 fits into 6, 3 times. Write 3.
2. $3 \times 2 = 6$. Write 6.
3. Subtract. $6 - 6 = 0$.
4. Bring down the next digit, which is 4.

```
      3
  2) 6,488
    -6 ↓
     0 4
```

Repeat this 4-step process until there are no more digits to "bring down". The result is $6{,}488 \div 2 = 3{,}244$.

```
     3,244
  2) 6,488
    -6
     0 4
     - 4
        08
       -8
         08
         -8
          0
```

Estimating Solutions

Problems involving addition, subtraction, multiplication, and division can be estimated before solving. Estimating before solving allows you to check an answer for **reasonableness**. For example, consider the problem $4{,}532 \div 8$. This can be estimated using compatible numbers. 4,532 is close to 4,500, and 8 is close to 9. These are considered **compatible numbers** because 4,500 can be quickly divided by 9.

$45 \div 9$ is 5.

$450 \div 9$ is 50.

$4{,}500 \div 9$ is 500.

This can be done using mental math, and this estimate can be compared to the "actual" answer. If the actual answer is close to 500, then the answer is likely correct.

$4{,}532 \div 8$ can be solved using long division:

```
          566  R4
  8)    4,532
     -  4 0
          53
        - 48
           52
          -48
            4
```

566 R4 is close to 500, so the answer is reasonable.

The reasonableness of an answer can be determined using estimation. For example, the product of 6,128 times 197 can be estimated quickly by rounding 6,128 to the nearest thousand, and rounding 197 to the nearest hundred.

6,128 becomes 6,000.

197 becomes 200.

$6{,}000 \times 200 = 1{,}200{,}000$

Remember, when rounding, first find the digit you are rounding, and then look to the digit to the right. If the digit to the right is 5 or more, the number rounds up. If the digit to the right is less than 5, the number stays the same.

For example, when rounding 6,284 to the nearest hundred, locate the digit in the hundreds place. 2 is in the hundreds place.

Now look to the right. The digit to the right of 2 is 8. 8 is 5 or more, so 2 will round up. 6,284 becomes 6,300. Notice how all digits to the right of the hundreds place become 0.

Solving Problems

You and 7 friends are washing cars to earn money. The car wash costs \$5, and so far, 20 cars have been washed. If the earnings are split equally, how much money has each person earned so far?

Recall multiplication facts. Each car pays \$5, and 20 cars have been washed. $5 \times 2 = 10$, so $5 \times 20 = 100$. \$100 has been earned so far.

There are 8 friends in the group altogether. $100 \div 8$ can be solved using long division.

```
   12 R4
8) 100
  -8
   20
  -16
    4
```

There is a remainder of 4. To express R4 in terms of money, start by writing the remainder as a fraction. R4 means $\frac{4}{8}$.

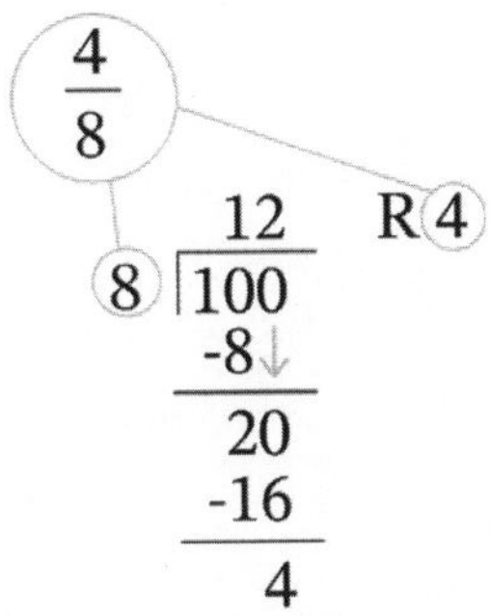

$\frac{4}{8}$ simplifies to $\frac{1}{2}$, which is the decimal 0.50. In terms of money, 0.50 is 50 cents. So, R4 represents 50 cents. Each person has earned \$12.50 so far.

Example

An artist sold 8 paintings at a craft fair. Each painting sold for \$16. The artist divided the earnings into 5 equal groups. How much money is in each group?

The scenario can be converted from word from to numeral form:

$$(16 \times 8) \div 5$$

Perform the operation in the parentheses first.

$$16 \times 8 = 128$$

Now divide 128 into 5 equal groups.

$$128 \div 5 = 25 \text{ r } 3$$

```
   25r3
5) 128
  -10
    28
   -25
     3
```

So,

$$128 \div 5 = 25 \text{ r } 3$$

In this case, remainder 3 means $\frac{3}{5}$ because the artist is dividing the money into 5 groups. $\frac{3}{5}$ is equivalent to $\frac{6}{10}$ or 0.6.

This means $128 \div 5 = 25.6$. The amount of money in each group is \$25.60.

Example

Mark has 3 boxes of cupcake mix. Each box makes 20 cupcakes. When Mark bakes the cupcakes, he can fit 10 cupcakes in each pan. If Mark uses the pan to make one batch of cupcakes at a time, how many times will he use the pan?

3 boxes that make 20 cupcakes each means 60 cupcakes: $3 \times 20 = 60$.

60 cupcakes are baked using 1 pan. Each pan holds 10 cupcakes, so divide 60 by 10: $60 \div 10 = 6$. This means the pan needs to be used 6 times.

Input-Output Tables

Expressions, such as $5m$, can be displayed in an **input-output table**. For example, in the expression $5m$, when $m = 1$, the expression becomes $5(1)$ which simplifies to 5. When $m = 2$, the expression becomes $5(2)$ which simplifies to 10. The pattern continues.

This can be shown with an input-output table. The **input value** is m, and the **output value** is determined when the expression is evaluated.

Input (m)	1	2	3	4	5
Output ($5m$)	5	10	15	20	25

Notice how each input value increases by 1, and each output value increases by 5.

When an input-output table represents a consistent pattern, the pattern is referred to as a **rule**. The rule in this example is, "multiply by five." A rule makes it possible to determine unknown values in an input-output table. For example, if $m = 15$, the output is determined by multiplying 15 and 5: $15 \times 5 = 75$. When $m = 5$, the output is 75.

Example

Complete the input-output table relating the number of bikes and the total number of wheels. Write a rule to describe the relationship.

Number of Bikes	Number of Wheels
1	2
2	
4	
6	
10	

The relationship between the number of bikes and the number of wheels can be described with the following "rule": $w = 2b$, where w represents the total number of wheels, and b represents the number of bikes. The total number of wheels is calculated by multiplying the number of bikes by 2.

Number of Bikes	Number of Wheels
1	2
2	4
4	8
6	12
10	20

EXAMPLE

Complete the input-output table based on the following rule. RULE: Add 19 to the input.

Input	Output
4	
9	
16	
19	
25	

The rule states "add 19 to the input". This means that 19 will be added to every input value to calculate the corresponding output value.

Input	Output
4	23
9	28
16	35
19	38
25	44

Number Sense and Operations with Fractions and Decimals

Decimals

Representing Decimals with Models

It can be helpful to **visualize** fractions and decimals as a **model**. For example, when one whole is divided into 10 equal shares, each share represents 1 out of 10. As a fraction this is $\frac{1}{10}$, and as a decimal this is 0.1.

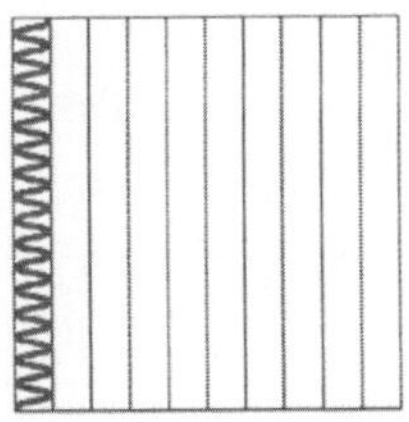

When one whole is divided into 100 equal shares, each share represents 1 out of 100. As a fraction this is $\frac{1}{100}$, and as a decimal this is 0.01.

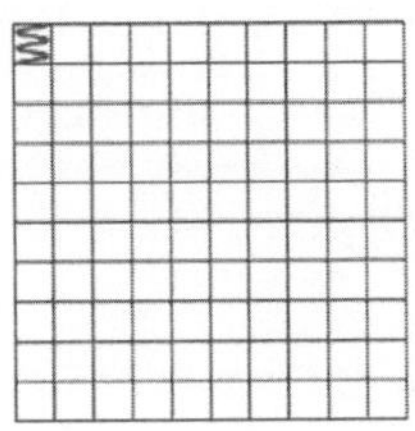

Notice how 1 out of 10 is the same amount as 10 out of 100. So, $\frac{1}{10}$ and $\frac{10}{100}$ are considered equivalent fractions. This means 0.1 and 0.10 are considered equivalent decimals.

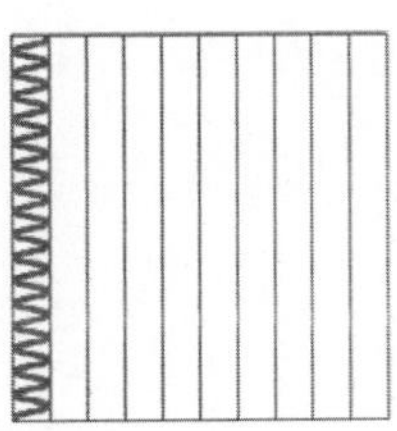

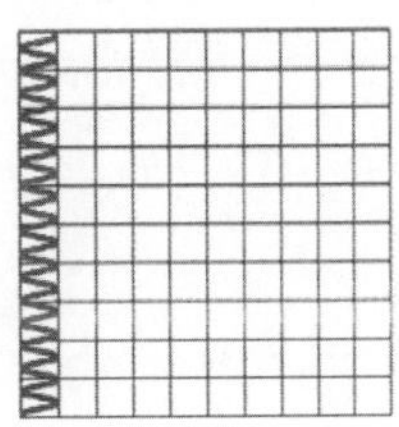

Comparing and Ordering Decimals

Decimals can be compared and ordered by **comparing each digit** from left to right. For example, 13.84 and 13.54 have the same digit in the tens place (1), the same digit in the ones place (3), but they have a different digit in the tenths place. Comparing these values, we see $8 > 5$, which means 13.84 is greater than 13.54.

This can also be seen using a visual model. For example, when comparing decimals in a model, the larger decimal value will cover a larger portion of the whole. The model on the left shows 6 out of

10, or 0.6. The model on the right shows 13 out of 100, or 0.13. Notice how 0.6 has a larger shaded region. This means 0.6 is greater than 0.13.

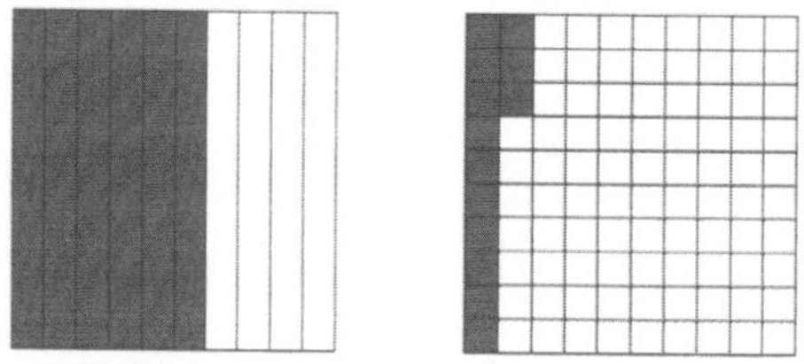

It is important to be aware of the **place value** when comparing decimal values. For example, consider the place value when comparing 0.3 and 0.03. Both values contain a 3, but one represents 3 tenths and the other represents 3 hundredths. Notice how $\frac{3}{10}$ covers more of the model than $\frac{3}{100}$.

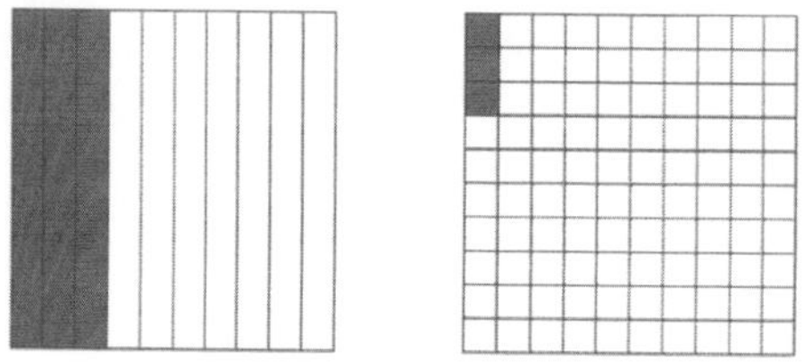

Decimals on a Number Line

A number line is a great way to visualize decimals to the tenths or the hundredths places. On a number line, tenths show 10 equal segments from 0 to 1. Notice how the hash marks increase by 0.1 from left to right. The left dot is on the third hash mark, so it represents 0.3 or $\frac{3}{10}$. The right dot is on the ninth hash mark, so it represents 0.9 or $\frac{9}{10}$.

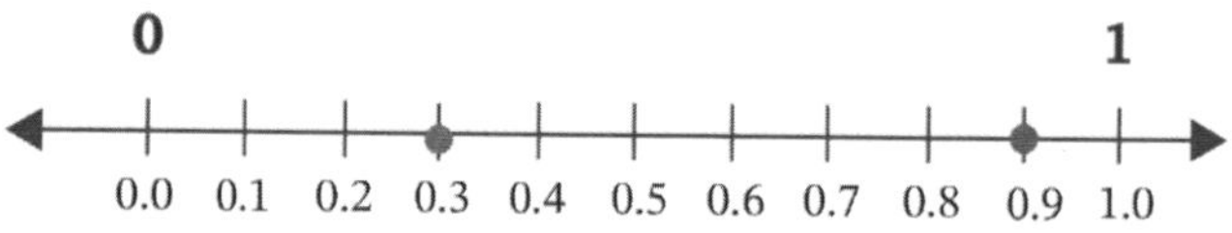

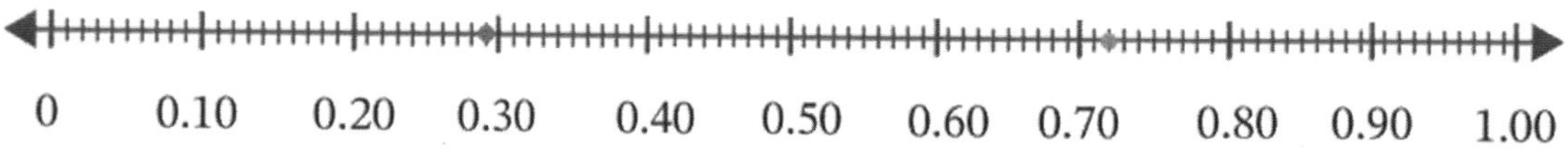

Hundredths show 100 equal segments from 0 to 100.

The left dot is on the 29th hash mark, so it represents $\frac{29}{100}$. The fraction $\frac{29}{100}$ as a decimal is 0.29. The orange dot is on the 72nd hash mark, so it represents $\frac{72}{100}$. The fraction $\frac{72}{100}$ as a decimal is 0.72.

Representing Decimals with Money

Money is expressed in **dollars** and **cents**. Cents are represented as **tenths** and **hundredths**. For example, $4.92 represents 4 whole dollars, 9 tenths of a dollar, and 2 hundredths of a dollar.

Express the coins as a decimal dollar amount:

4 quarters, 4 nickels, 2 pennies.

4 quarters: $\$0.25 + \$0.25 + \$0.25 + \$0.25 = \$1.00$

4 nickels: $\$0.05 + \$0.05 + \$0.05 + \$0.05 = \$0.20$

2 pennies: $\$0.01 + \$0.01 = \$0.02$

Remember, line up the decimal points when adding decimals.

$$\begin{array}{r} 1.\ 00 \\ 0.\ 20 \\ +0.\ 02 \\ \hline \$1.\ 22 \end{array}$$

Example

Consider the model below. What fraction would this represent? What decimal? What dollar amount?

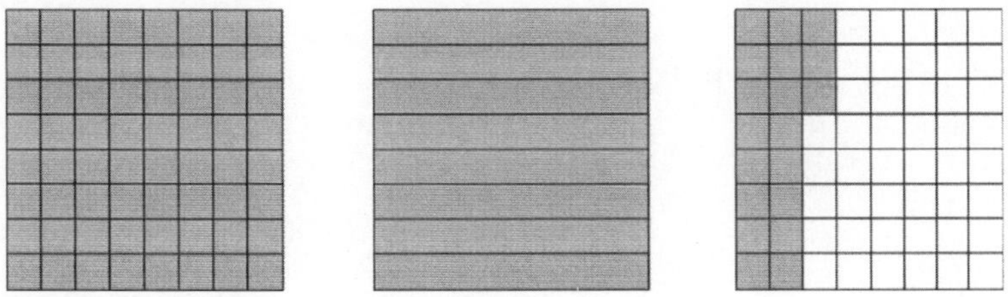

The model shows $\frac{100}{100} + \frac{10}{10} + \frac{23}{100}$.

This represents 2 wholes and 23 hundredths.

As a decimal, this is 2.23.

As a dollar amount, this represents \$2.23.

Adding and Subtracting Decimals and Whole Numbers

The important thing to remember when adding and subtracting decimal numbers is to **line up** the **decimal points**. Lining up the decimal points ensures that similar place values are being combined. For example, ones combine with ones, tens combine with tens.

Consider the following: A pizza costs \$27.50 and a drink costs \$4.65. The total cost of the meal can be calculated by finding the sum. Stack the numbers vertically and line up the decimal points. With addition, it does not matter which number is on top or bottom. Regroup if necessary and bring the decimal straight down into the answer line. This method is known as the **standard algorithm**.

$$\begin{array}{r} 11 \\ 27.\ 50 \\ +\ \ 4.\ 65 \\ \hline \$32.\ 15 \end{array}$$

The standard algorithm is also useful for subtraction scenarios. For example, if a piece of ribbon measures 132.1 centimeters, and 27.76 centimeters are cut off and removed, how many centimeters of ribbon are left?

Stack the values vertically and line up the decimals. Make sure the larger number, 132.1, is on the top. Sometimes it is helpful to fill in any empty spaces with a zero. Regroup if necessary, and again bring the decimal straight down into the answer line.

$$\begin{array}{rrrcrr} & & 11 & & 10 & \\ & 2 & \not{1} & & \not{0} & 10 \\ 1 & \not{3} & \not{2} & . & \not{1} & \not{0} \\ - & 2 & 7 & . & 7 & 6 \\ \hline 1 & 0 & 4 & . & 3 & 4 \end{array}$$

There are 104.34 centimeters of ribbon left.

Review Video: Adding and Subtracting Decimals
Visit mometrix.com/academy and enter code: 381101

Example

Solve using the standard algorithm: $40.03 - 26.12 =$ ____

Line up the decimals when adding and subtracting decimals. Regrouping is required for this problem.

$$\begin{array}{rrcrr} & 9 & & & \\ 3 & \not{10} & & 10 & \\ \not{4} & \not{0} & . & \not{0} & 3 \\ -2 & 6 & . & 1 & 2 \\ \hline 1 & 3 & . & 9 & 1 \end{array}$$

$$40.03 - 26.12 = 13.91$$

Check for accuracy using addition: $13.91 + 26.12 = 40.03$.

Example

Solve using the standard algorithm: $63.04 + 99.09 =$ ____.

$$\begin{array}{rrrcrr} & 1 & & & 1 & \\ & 6 & 3 & . & 0 & 4 \\ + & 9 & 9 & . & 0 & 9 \\ \hline 1 & 6 & 2 & . & 1 & 3 \end{array}$$

Line up the decimals when adding and subtracting decimals: $63.04 + 99.09 = 162.13$.

Relating Decimals to Fractions

Converting Decimals to Fractions

Decimals and fractions can be used to represent values less than one whole. Remember, one decimal place value to the right of the decimal point represents tenths, and two decimal places to the right of the decimal point represents hundredths. For example, 0.4 represents 4 tenths, or as a fraction $\frac{4}{10}$. The number 0.04 represents 4 hundredths, or as a fraction $\frac{4}{100}$.

When a decimal extends to the tenths place, the fraction has a denominator of 10.

$$0.1 = \frac{1}{10}$$

$$0.2 = \frac{2}{10}$$

$$0.3 = \frac{3}{10}$$

$$0.4 = \frac{4}{10}$$

When a decimal extends to the hundredths place, the fraction has a denominator of 100.

$$0.45 = \frac{45}{100}$$

$$0.35 = \frac{35}{100}$$

$$0.25 = \frac{25}{100}$$

$$0.15 = \frac{15}{100}$$

Equivalent Decimals and Fractions

Notice how $\frac{40}{100}$ and $\frac{4}{10}$ cover the **same amount** of the model. This means that $\frac{40}{100}$ and $\frac{4}{10}$ are **equivalent** fractions. Since $\frac{40}{100}$ and $\frac{4}{10}$ are equivalent fractions, 0.40 and 0.4 are equivalent decimals.

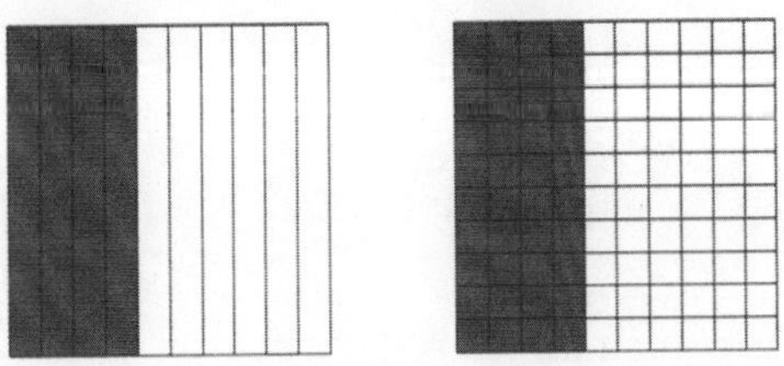

Here are some other examples of equivalent fractions and decimals:

$$\frac{1}{10} = 0.1 = 0.10 = \frac{10}{100}$$

$$\frac{2}{10} = 0.2 = 0.20 = \frac{20}{100}$$

$$\frac{3}{10} = 0.3 = 0.30 = \frac{30}{100}$$

Example

Express "45 hundredths" as a decimal and a fraction in simplest form.

45 hundredths represents 45 out of 100, which as a fraction is $\frac{45}{100}$. This fraction can be simplified. 45 and 100 have a factor in common. Divide both the numerator and denominator by the common factor of 5. $\frac{45}{100}$ becomes $\frac{9}{20}$.

$\frac{45}{100}$ can be expressed as a decimal. $\frac{45}{100}$ can be thought of as 4 tenths plus 5 hundredths. $\frac{4}{10}$ and $\frac{5}{100}$ is expressed as 0.45 in decimal form: $\frac{45}{100} = 0.45$.

45 hundredths as a decimal and a fraction: 0.45 and $\frac{9}{20}$.

Example

Draw lines to connect the fraction and decimal values that are equivalent.

0.7	$\frac{6}{100}$
$\frac{2}{100}$	0.8
0.06	0.99
$\frac{99}{100}$	$\frac{7}{10}$
$\frac{4}{5}$	0.02

0.7 represents 7 tenths. As a fraction 0.7 is $\frac{7}{10}$.

$\frac{2}{100}$ represents 2 hundredths. As a decimal $\frac{2}{100}$ is 0.02.

0.06 represents 6 hundredths. As a fraction 0.06 is $\frac{6}{100}$.

$\frac{99}{100}$ represents 99 hundredths. As a decimal $\frac{99}{100}$ is 0.99.

$\frac{4}{5}$ represents 4 fifths, or 8 tenths. As a decimal $\frac{4}{5}$ is 0.8.

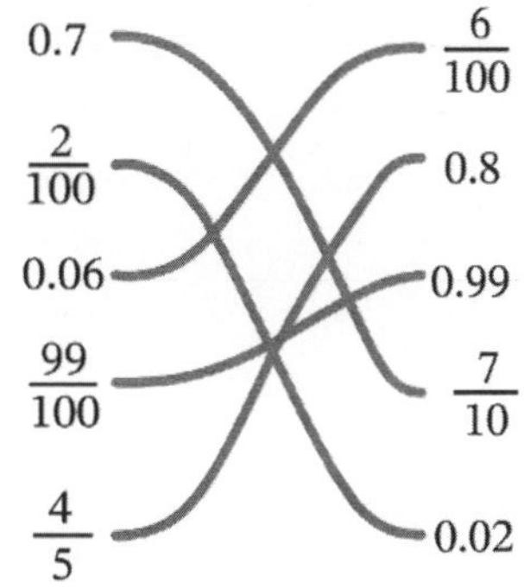

Fractions

Values that are greater than 0 but less than or equal to 1 can be represented as a **fraction**. For example, the pizza, watermelon, and lemon are each sliced into equal pieces. The pizza has 6 equal pieces, the watermelon has 4 equal pieces, and the lemon has 8 equal pieces. These values represent the denominator of a fraction. Remember, the **denominator** is the bottom number in a fraction, which represents the **total number of pieces**.

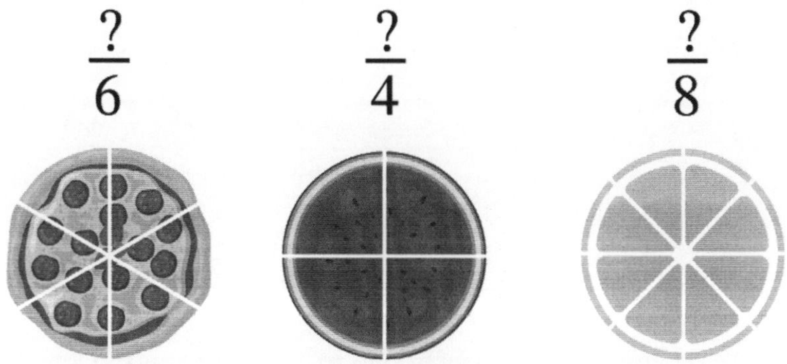

If 3 slices of each food are eaten, 3 would be the **numerator**.

$\frac{3}{6}$ of the pizza is eaten. $\frac{3}{4}$ of the watermelon is eaten. $\frac{3}{8}$ of the lemon is eaten.

Fractions can also be modeled using number lines or **fraction strips**.

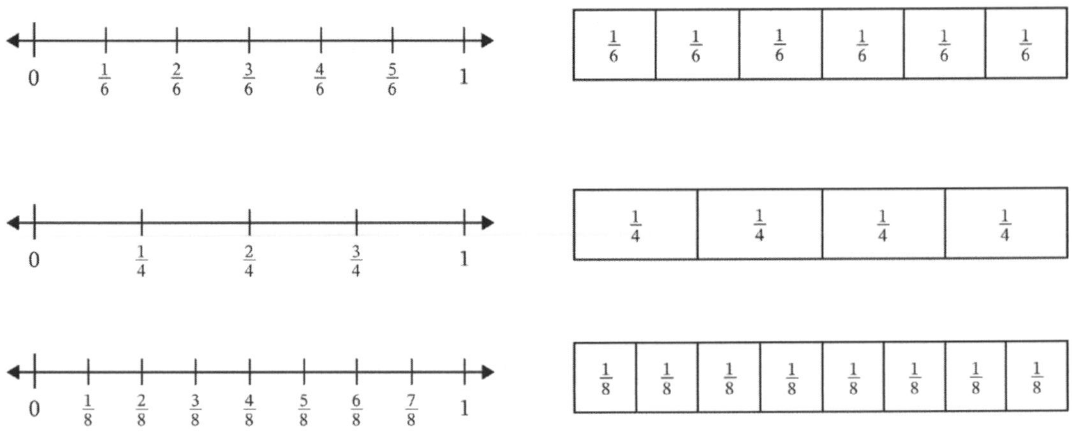

Fractions and Number Lines

Fractions are often displayed using models, fraction strips, pictures, or number lines. When determining a fraction from a number line, check to see how many **parts** there are within **one whole**. For example, consider the number line below. Notice how there are 4 **equal parts** from 0 to 1. This means each hash mark represents 1 out of 4, or $\frac{1}{4}$. Count up by $\frac{1}{4}$ to determine the missing value. $\frac{1}{4}, \frac{2}{4}, \frac{3}{4}$... The missing value is $\frac{3}{4}$.

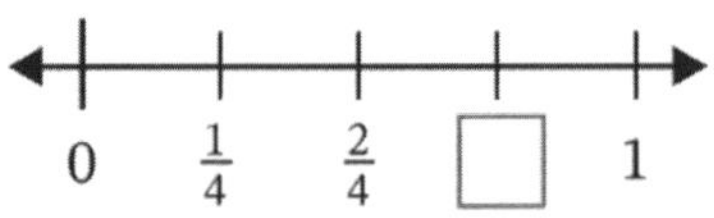

Consider the number line below. To identify the fraction that the green dot represents, first figure out the interval. The **interval** is essentially how many equal parts are shown to be within one whole number. In this case, there are 10 equal parts from 0 to 1. This means the interval is tenths. Starting from 0, or $\frac{0}{10}$, each hop to the right increases by $\frac{1}{10}$. The dot represents 8 hops, so $\frac{8}{10}$.

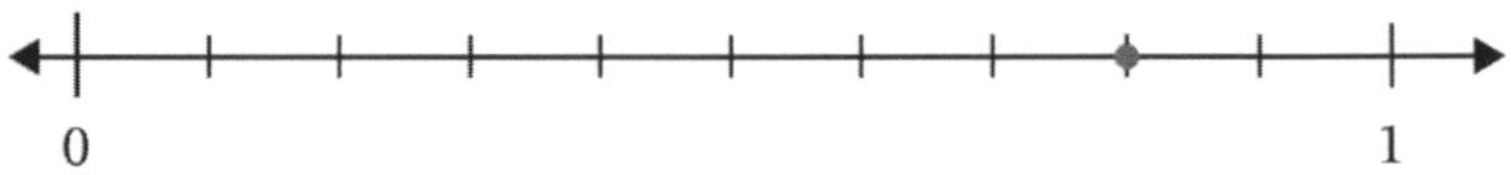

Unit Fractions

A **unit fraction** is any fraction with a numerator of 1. For example, $\frac{1}{2}, \frac{1}{3}, \frac{1}{4}$, and $\frac{1}{5}$ are considered unit fractions. When a unit fraction is added to itself multiple times, the result is a larger fraction. For example, $\frac{1}{8}+\frac{1}{8}+\frac{1}{8}=\frac{3}{8}$.

The opposite of this is **decomposing** a fraction into the sum of its unit fractions.

$\frac{5}{6}$ is the result of combining $\frac{1}{6}$ five times.

$$\frac{5}{6}=\frac{1}{6}+\frac{1}{6}+\frac{1}{6}+\frac{1}{6}+\frac{1}{6}$$

This is true for **mixed numbers** and **improper** fractions as well. Mixed numbers are values that are written using a whole number and a fraction. For example, $2\frac{1}{3}$ is a mixed number that consists of 7 groups of $\frac{1}{3}$.

$$2\frac{1}{3}=\frac{1}{3}+\frac{1}{3}+\frac{1}{3}+\frac{1}{3}+\frac{1}{3}+\frac{1}{3}+\frac{1}{3}$$

Improper fractions are fractions that have a numerator that is greater than the denominator. $\frac{4}{3}$ is an improper fraction that consists of 4 groups of $\frac{1}{3}$.

$$\frac{4}{3}=\frac{1}{3}+\frac{1}{3}+\frac{1}{3}+\frac{1}{3}$$

Decomposing Fractions

When a fraction is decomposed, it is **split up** into **smaller** fractions. The sum of these smaller fractions is the original fraction. For example, $\frac{7}{8}$ can be split up into the sum of $\frac{1}{8}+\frac{1}{8}+\frac{1}{8}+\frac{1}{8}+\frac{1}{8}+\frac{1}{8}+\frac{1}{8}$. However, this is not the only way to decompose $\frac{7}{8}$.

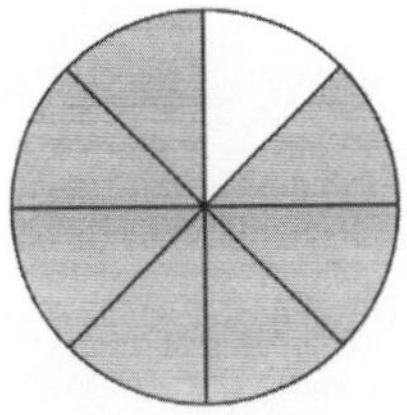

For example, the model below shows 7 shaded shares out of 8, or the fraction $\frac{7}{8}$. The fraction $\frac{7}{8}$ can be created in many ways. For example, $\frac{2}{8}+\frac{4}{8}+\frac{1}{8}$ has a sum of $\frac{7}{8}$.

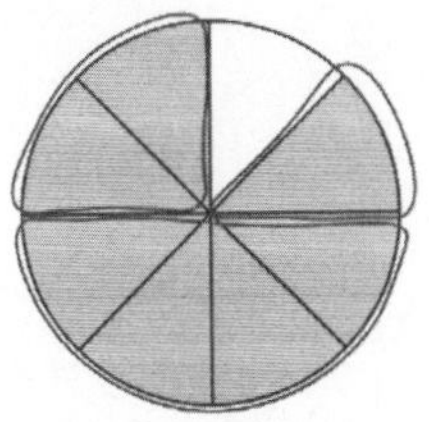

Equivalent Fractions

Fractions are considered **equivalent** if they represent the same amount. There are a few ways to determine if fractions are equivalent.

Models

Fractions can be compared by drawing a quick sketch. For example, consider the fractions $\frac{6}{8}$ and $\frac{3}{4}$. Create two circles that are the same size. Divide one circle into 8 equal shares, and the other circle into 4 equal shares. Notice how 6 out of 8 is the same size as 3 out of 4. Since $\frac{6}{8}$ and $\frac{3}{4}$ cover the same amount of each circle, they are considered equivalent. Creating a sketch or a model is a great way to compare fractions with denominators that are small. However, when denominators are larger, like $\frac{1}{40}$ or $\frac{39}{100}$, a sketch is unreasonable.

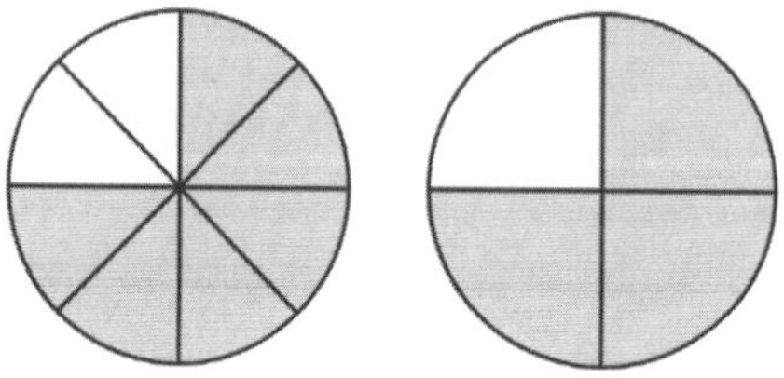

Common Denominators

For larger denominators, consider using a common denominator to determine if fractions are equivalent. For example, consider the fractions $\frac{46}{100}$ and $\frac{70}{150}$. The fractions cannot be compared until they have the same denominator. The lowest common multiple of 100 and 150 is 300. Set up each fraction with 300 as the denominator.

$\frac{46}{100}$ becomes $\frac{x}{300}$.

$\frac{70}{150}$ becomes $\frac{y}{300}$.

Now adjust the numerators.

$\frac{46}{100}$: The denominator is multiplied by 3 to get 300, so multiply the numerator by 3 as well: $\frac{46\times3}{100\times3} = \frac{138}{300}$.

$\frac{70}{150}$: The denominator is multiplied by 2 to get 300, so multiply the numerator by 2 as well: $\frac{70\times2}{150\times2} = \frac{140}{300}$.

Now that the two fractions have the same denominator, they can be compared. $\frac{138}{300}$ is not equivalent to $\frac{140}{300}$ because the numerators are different while the denominators are the same.

Comparing Fractions

It can be difficult to compare fractions when the numerators and denominators are different. For example, consider the fractions $\frac{7}{9}$ and $\frac{8}{11}$. It is difficult to know which fraction is larger because one fraction is out of 9, and one fraction is out of 11. To compare these fractions, create a common denominator.

One denominator is 9, and the other is 11. A common denominator can be calculated by determining the least common multiple (LCM). The LCM of 9 and 11 is 99. Set up each fraction with 99 as the new denominator.

$\frac{7}{9}$ becomes $\frac{x}{99}$ and $\frac{8}{11}$ becomes $\frac{x}{99}$.

Now adjust the numerators.

The denominator in $\frac{7}{9}$ was multiplied by 11 to reach $\frac{x}{99}$. Multiply the numerator by 11 as well: $\frac{7\times11}{9\times11} = \frac{77}{99}$.

The denominator in $\frac{8}{11}$ was multiplied by 9 to reach $\frac{x}{99}$. Multiply the numerator by 9 as well: $\frac{8\times9}{11\times9} = \frac{72}{99}$.

Now the two new fractions can be compared. $\frac{77}{99}$ is greater than $\frac{72}{99}$, or $\frac{77}{99} > \frac{72}{99}$.

Example

Fill in the blank to make the statement true. $\frac{3}{5}$ __ $\frac{2}{7}$

Use one of the following symbols: >, <, or =.

$\frac{3}{5}$ and $\frac{2}{7}$ have different denominators. To compare the fractions, rewrite each fraction with a common denominator. The lowest multiple that both 5 and 7 have in common is 35. Rewrite the fractions with 35 as the denominator.

$\frac{3}{5}$ becomes $\frac{?}{35}$

$\frac{2}{7}$ becomes $\frac{?}{35}$

Now adjust the numerators.

$\frac{3}{5}$: The denominator was 5 and now it is 35. 5 was multiplied by 7, so multiply the numerator by 7 as well. $\frac{3}{5}$ becomes $\frac{21}{35}$.

$\frac{2}{7}$: The denominator was 7 and now it is 35. 7 was multiplied by 5, so multiply the numerator by 5 as well. $\frac{2}{7}$ becomes $\frac{10}{35}$.

$\frac{21}{35} > \frac{10}{35}$, therefore $\frac{3}{5} > \frac{2}{7}$.

EXAMPLE

Compare the two fractions using the symbol >,<, or =: $\frac{5}{6}$ __ $\frac{7}{8}$.

The fractions $\frac{5}{6}$ and $\frac{7}{8}$ can be compared once they have a common denominator. Look at the denominators: 6 and 8. The lowest common multiple of 6 and 8 is 24. Make 24 the new denominator for both fractions.

$\frac{5}{6}$ becomes $\frac{?}{24}$

$\frac{7}{8}$ becomes $\frac{?}{24}$

Now adjust the numerators. What was the original denominator multiplied by? Multiply the numerator by this same amount.

$\frac{5}{6}$: The denominator was multiplied by 4 to create $\frac{?}{24}$. Multiply the numerator by 4. $\frac{5}{6}$ becomes $\frac{20}{24}$.

$\frac{7}{8}$: The denominator was multiplied by 3 to create $\frac{?}{24}$. Multiply the numerator by 3. $\frac{7}{8}$ becomes $\frac{21}{24}$.

$\frac{20}{24} < \frac{21}{24}$, therefore $\frac{5}{6} < \frac{7}{8}$.

ADDING AND SUBTRACTING FRACTIONS

Fractions represent part of a whole. Fractions with the same denominator can be combined by adding the parts (the numerators, or top numbers). This can be represented using a model. For example, the model below shows 3 parts out of 6, and 1 part out of 6. In other words, the whole model shows $\frac{3}{6} + \frac{1}{6}$.

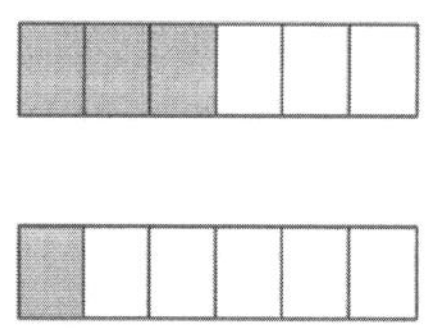

Both fractions consist of sixths, so the parts can be combined. 3 parts combined with 1 part equals 4 parts. 4 parts out of 6 parts represents the fraction $\frac{4}{6}$.

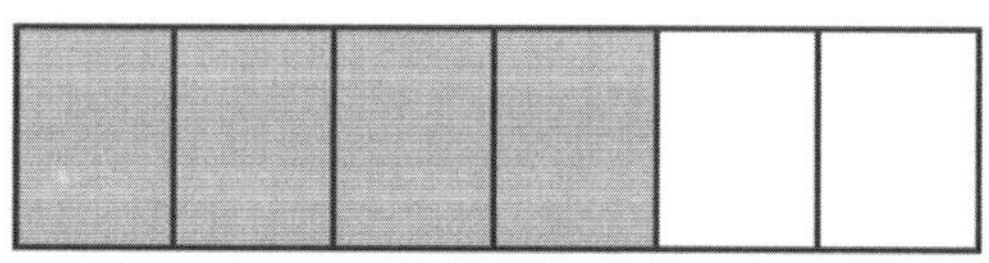

Try another example. Consider the diagram below. Each whole is divided into 8 equal shares. The circle on the left shows 2 out of 8, or $\frac{2}{8}$. The circle on the right shows 6 out of 8, or $\frac{6}{8}$.

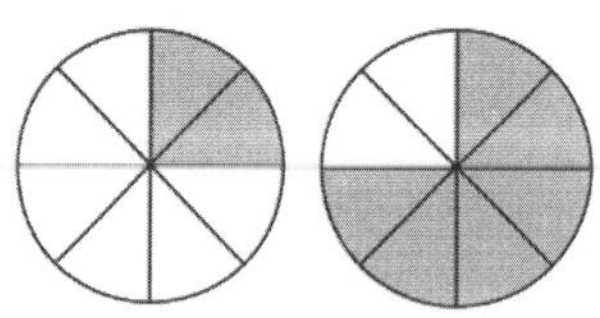

Both fractions have the same denominators so their numerators can be combined. $\frac{2}{8} + \frac{6}{8}$ combines to $\frac{8}{8}$. Another way to express $\frac{8}{8}$ is 1 whole.

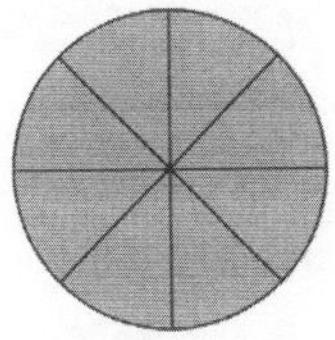

A picture or model is a great way to represent addition and subtraction of fractions. However, there is a shortcut! When denominators are the same, simply add or subtract the numerators.

$$\frac{2}{7} + \frac{4}{7} = \frac{6}{7}$$

Notice how the denominator, 7, stays the same and the numerators are added.

$$\frac{8}{9} - \frac{3}{9} = \frac{5}{9}$$

Notice how the denominator, 9, stays the same and the numerators are subtracted.

EXAMPLE

Write and solve an addition equation that represents adding the top fraction to the bottom fraction illustrated below.

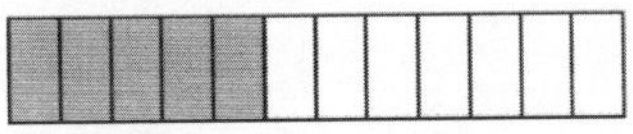

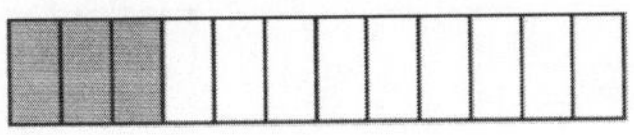

Top fraction: $\frac{5}{12}$

Bottom fraction: $\frac{3}{12}$

Both fractions have the same denominator, so they can be combined.

$$\frac{5}{12} + \frac{3}{12} = \frac{8}{12}$$

$\frac{8}{12}$ can be simplified by dividing the numerator and denominator by 4. $\frac{8}{12}$ becomes $\frac{2}{3}$.

$$\frac{5}{12} + \frac{3}{12} = \frac{8}{12} = \frac{2}{3}$$

Example

Model the subtraction equation on the number line, then solve: $\frac{6}{10} - \frac{2}{10} = ?$

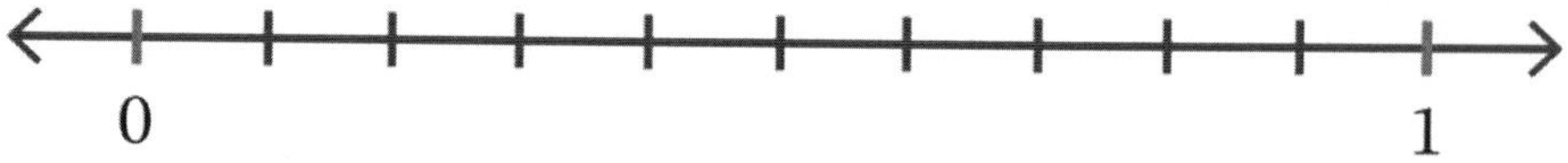

The number line is divided into 10 equal shares. Each hash mark represents $\frac{1}{10}$.

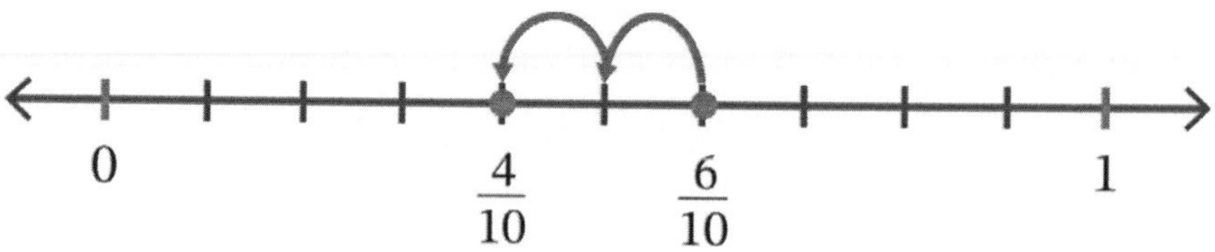

The red dot starts at $\frac{6}{10}$. The arrows show 2 jumps back, which represents subtraction of $\frac{2}{10}$: $\frac{6}{10} - \frac{2}{10} = \frac{4}{10}$.

Reasonable Sums and Differences of Fractions

One way to check whether or not the sums and differences of fractions are reasonable is to use benchmark fractions. **Benchmarks fractions** are common, easy to visualize fractions such as 0, $\frac{1}{4}$, $\frac{1}{2}$, $\frac{3}{4}$, and 1.

For example, consider the following addition equation:

$$\frac{1}{12} + \frac{7}{12} = \frac{8}{12}$$

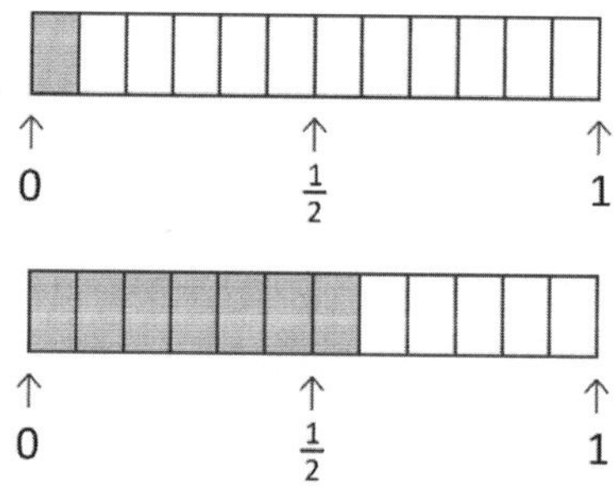

Notice how $\frac{1}{12}$ is close to the benchmark fraction 0, and $\frac{7}{12}$ is close to the benchmark fraction $\frac{1}{2}$. Since $0 + \frac{1}{2} = \frac{1}{2}$, the sum of $\frac{1}{12}$ and $\frac{7}{12}$ should be close to $\frac{1}{2}$.

$\frac{1}{12} + \frac{7}{12} = \frac{8}{12}$, and $\frac{8}{12}$ is close to $\frac{1}{2}$ since it's only one more shaded square from our picture earlier, so the sum is reasonable.

The same concept works for fractions with unequal denominators. For example, $\frac{7}{10} - \frac{2}{8} = \frac{9}{20}$. The reasonableness of the answer can be determined without solving the problem. From our picture, we can see that $\frac{7}{10}$ is close to $\frac{3}{4}$, and $\frac{2}{8}$ is the same as $\frac{1}{4}$. Therefore, the difference should be close to $\frac{3}{4} - \frac{1}{4}$ which is $\frac{2}{4}$, or $\frac{1}{2}$.

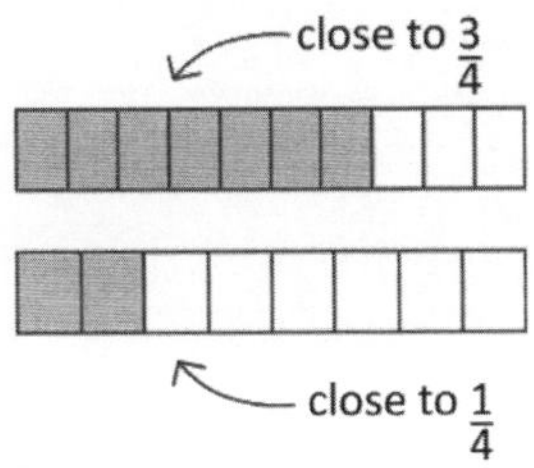

The equation shows $\frac{7}{10} - \frac{2}{8} = \frac{9}{20}$, and $\frac{9}{20}$ is very close to $\frac{2}{4}$ or $\frac{1}{2}$, so the answer seems to be reasonable.

Multiplying Fractions and Whole Numbers

Modeling strategies can be helpful when multiplying a whole number by a fraction. For example, $4 \times \frac{2}{3}$ can be thought of as 4 groups of $\frac{2}{3}$. There are 8 thirds altogether, so $4 \times \frac{2}{3} = \frac{8}{3}$, or as a mixed number, $2\frac{2}{3}$.

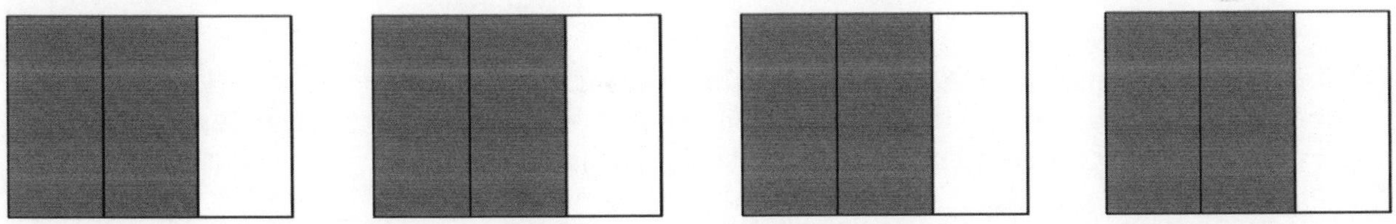

Multiplication is commutative, meaning the order does not matter. This same modeling strategy applies in situations where the fraction is listed first and the whole number is listed second.

Decimals and Fractions on a Number Line

Fractions with a denominator of 10 can be represented as a decimal value to the tenths place. For example, $\frac{9}{10}$ written as a decimal is 0.9.

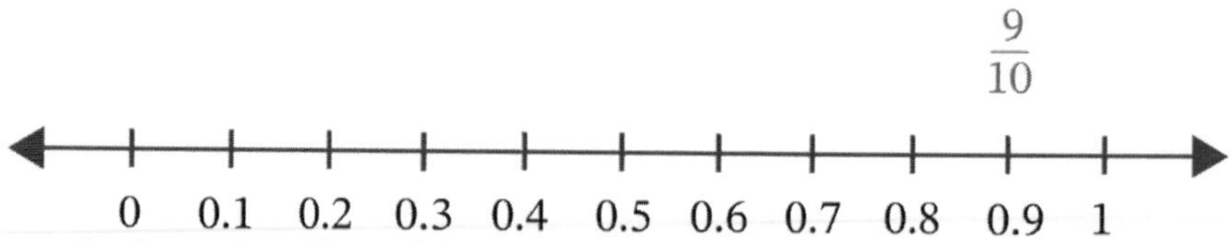

Similarly, fractions with a denominator of 100 can be represented as a decimal value to the hundredth place. For example, $\frac{9}{100}$ is 0.09 as a decimal.

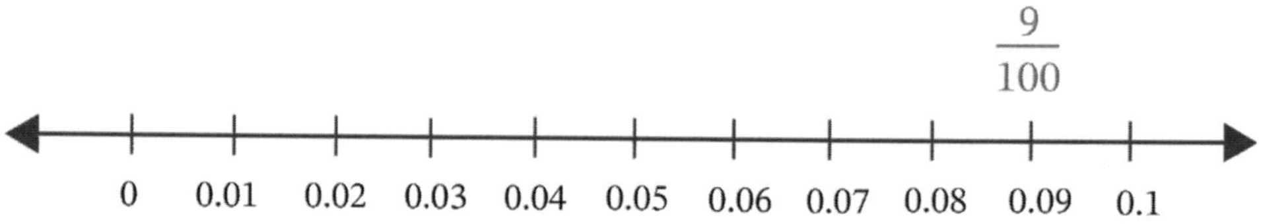

Decimals and fractions can be thought of as distances from zero on a number line. In general, the number line will extend from 0 to 1, where 1 represents 1 whole. Decimal and fraction values often represent values that are greater than 0 but less than 1 whole.

When a number line is not labeled, look for the number of equal segments. The number line below has 10 equal segments, which means each hash mark represents $\frac{1}{10}$. The dot is located on the eighth hash mark, so it represents $\frac{8}{10}$. The fraction $\frac{8}{10}$ represents the decimal 0.8 or 0.80. These values, $\frac{8}{10}$, 0.8, and 0.80, all represent the distance from zero.

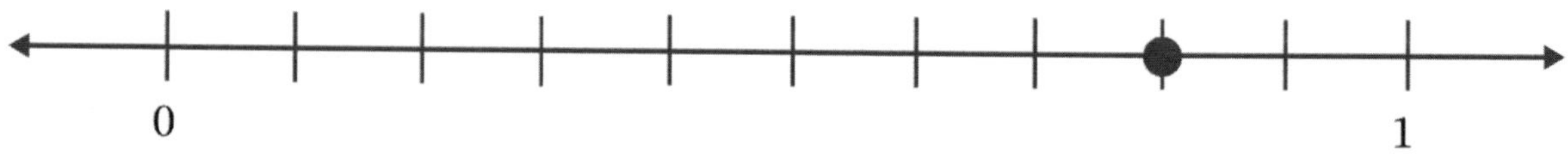

Geometric Reasoning, Measurement, and Data Analysis and Probability

Geometry Terms

Geometry, or the study of shapes, is filled with unique terminology and vocabulary. It is important to become familiar with this math vocabulary to be able to precisely classify and identify two- and three-dimensional shapes.

The most basic terms include points, lines, line segments, rays, angles, perpendicular lines, and parallel lines.

A **point** is an exact location with no size. This often appears as a dot, and is usually labeled with a letter, such as Point A.

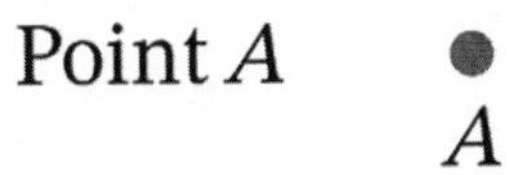

A **line** is a straight path that extends in opposite directions. A line does not have a width, and it extends indefinitely in both directions. Lines are labeled with letters representing points on the line, such as $\overleftrightarrow{AB}$.

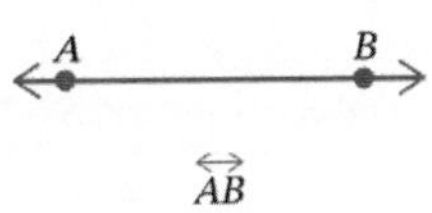

A **line segment** is a part of a line. A line segment has endpoints, beginning and ending at a point labeled with a letter, such as $\overline{AB}$.

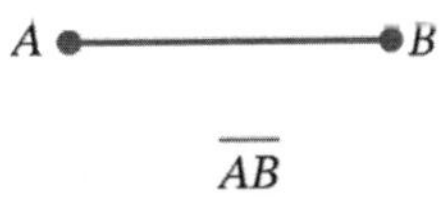

A **ray** is a part of a line that starts at an endpoint and then extends out indefinitely. Rays are labeled starting with a letter at the endpoint and ending with a letter representing another point on the ray, such as $\overrightarrow{AB}$.

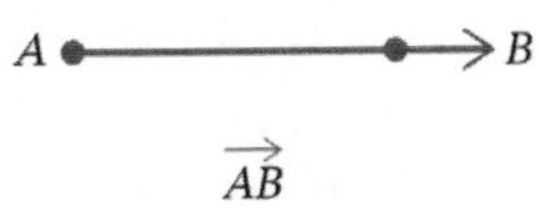

An **angle** is formed when two straight lines or rays meet at a common endpoint. The two rays below form an angle.

Parallel lines extend side-by-side and never intersect. To help visualize parallel lines, think of train tracks.

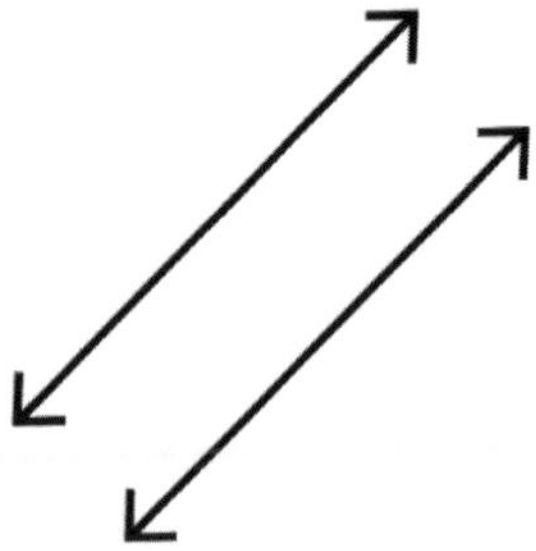

Perpendicular lines intersect to form a right angle. To help visualize perpendicular lines, think of a corner or a T-shape.

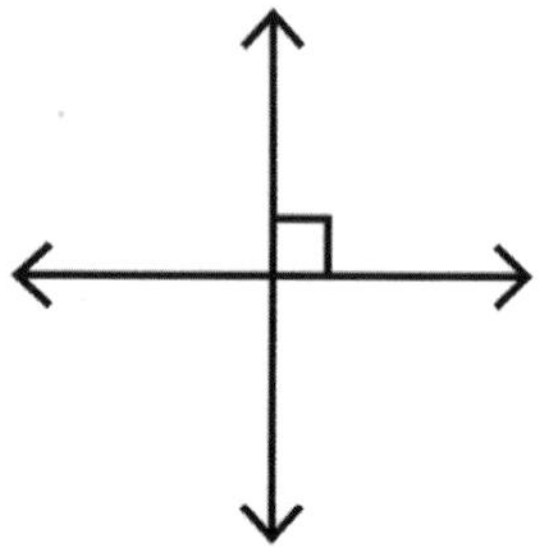

Review Video: Parallel and Perpendicular Lines
Visit mometrix.com/academy and enter code: 815923

Right, Acute, and Obtuse Angles

A **right angle** consists of 90 degrees and forms a corner. Angles that are less than 90 degrees are considered **acute angles**. Angles that are wider than 90 degrees but less than 180 degrees are considered **obtuse angles**.

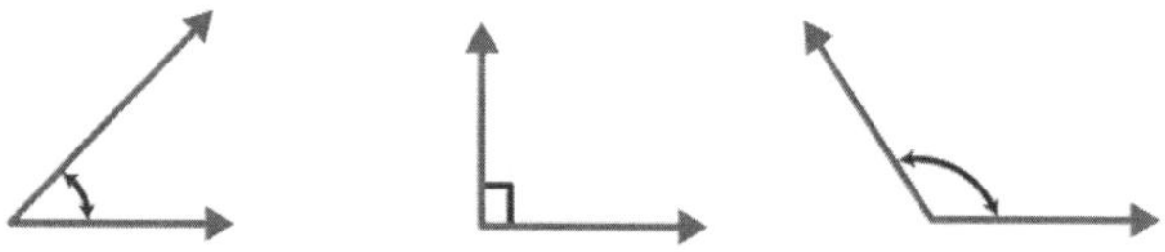

Acute angle | Right angle | Obtuse angle

Triangles can be built from acute, obtuse, or right angles. For example, a triangle with only acute angles is referred to as an **acute triangle**. A triangle with an obtuse angle is called an **obtuse triangle**. A triangle containing a right angle is called a **right triangle**.

Triangle 1 contains a 90-degree angle, so it is classified as a right triangle. This can be verified using a protractor. Triangle 2 contains three acute angles, so it is classified as an acute triangle. Triangle 3 contains an obtuse angle, so it is an obtuse triangle.

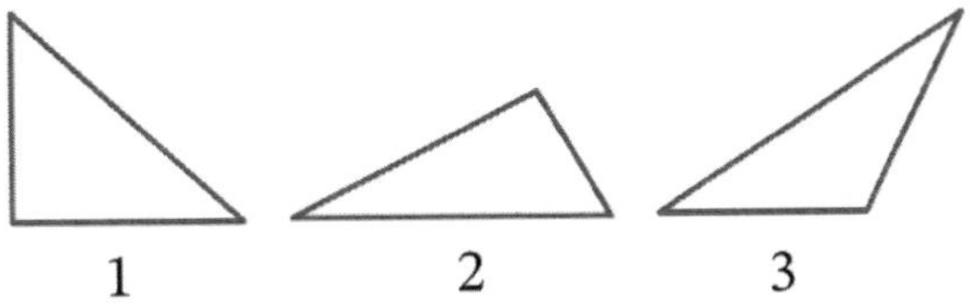

Measuring Angles

A **protractor** is a tool that is used to measure the **exact degree measure** of any angle. A protractor has two rows of degree measures, an inside row and an outside row. It is important to remember to use the row that starts at 0° when measuring angles. The row that is selected depends on the direction the angle opens. For example, notice how the protractor on the left shows an angle that opens to the right. The baseline on the right starts at 0° using the inside row of numbers. In contrast, the protractor on the right shows an angle that opens to the left. The baseline on the left starts at 0° using the outside row of numbers.

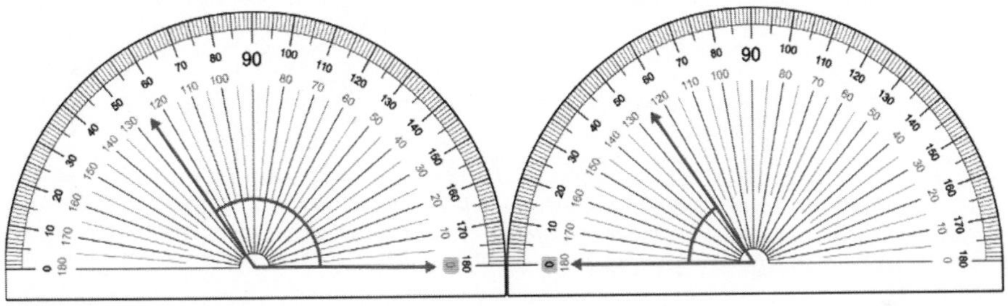

When using a protractor to measure an angle, identify the row of degree measures that start at 0°, and build the angle from there. For example, the angle below is built from two rays. The mouth of the angle opens to the right, so the inside row of numbers will be used. Starting at 0°, the angle extends all the way to 65°.

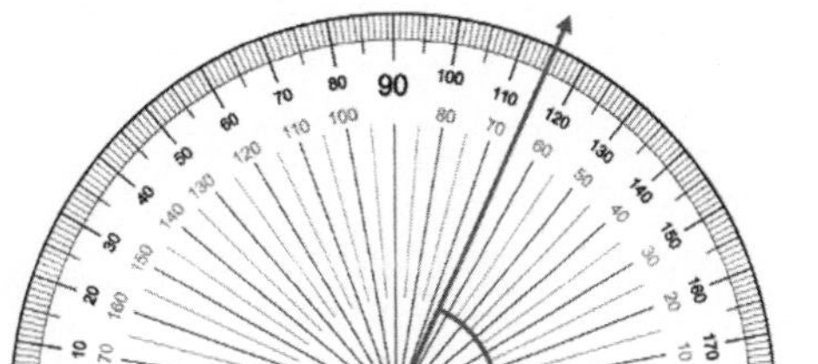

EXAMPLE

Use a protractor to determine the angle measure below.

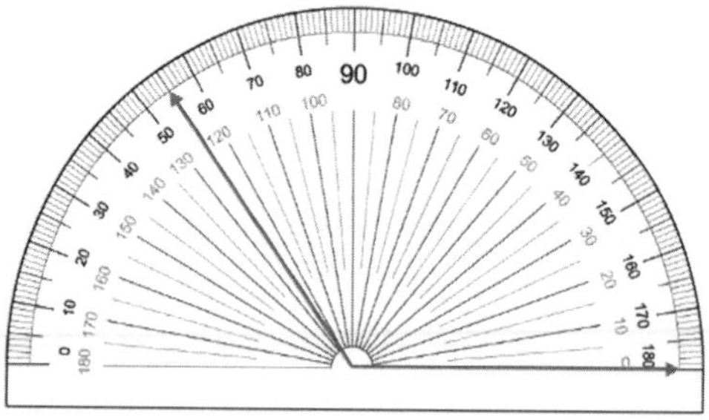

A protractor can be used to measure the obtuse angle. The angle is 125°.

EXAMPLE

Is the following angle greater or less than 85°?

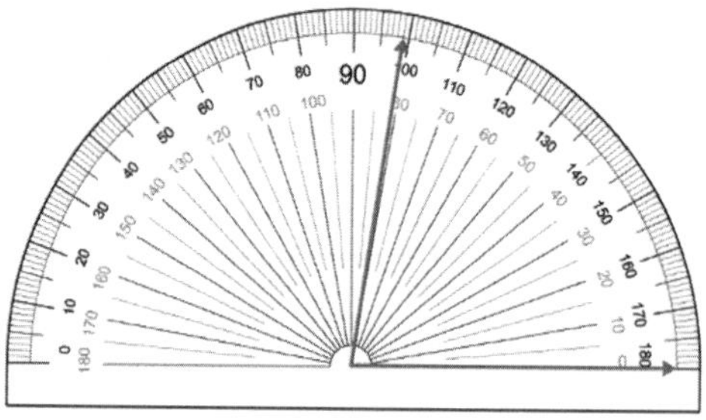

Less than. The angle above is an 81° angle.

Solving for Unknown Angle Measurements

When an unknown angle is formed from a **benchmark angle**, such as 180° or 90°, **subtraction** can be used to determine the missing angle. For example, the angle below shows a 90° angle formed by two adjacent angles. The sum of the 40° angle and the unknown angle need to combine to form a 90° angle.

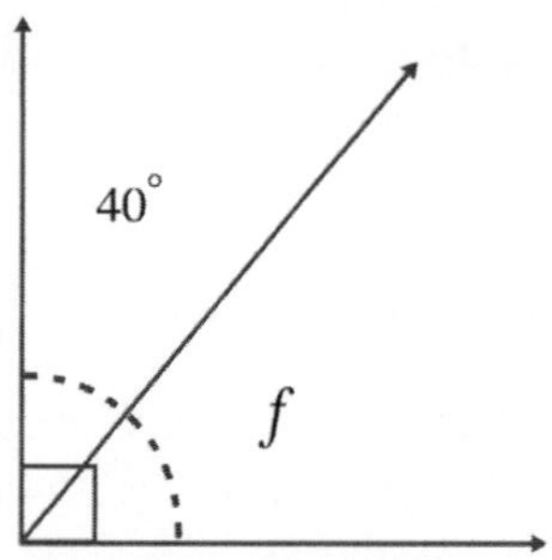

$$f = 90° - 40° = 50°$$

Adjacent angles won't always combine to form benchmark angles. For example, the adjacent angles below don't combine to form a benchmark angle. However, both angles combine to 120°. This means that angle $\angle a + \angle b = 120°$. $\angle a$ is 62°, so an addition equation can be set up.

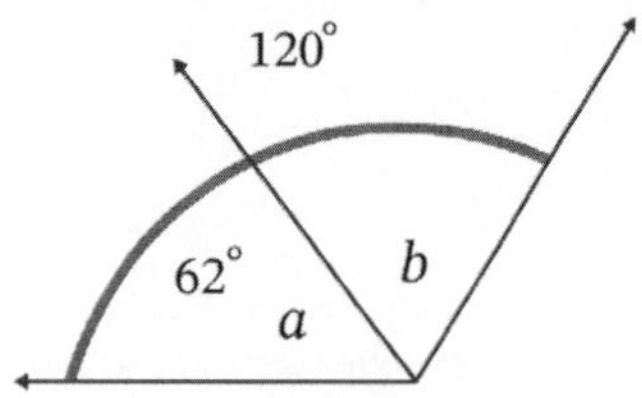

$$b = 120° - 62°$$
$$b = 58°$$

Relative Sizes of Measurements

The **metric system** is a system of measurement used for identifying mass, volume, and length. Most countries in the world use the metric system when making calculations in math and science. However, the United States has another measurement system called the **customary system**. The customary system also measures mass, volume, and length, but it uses different units.

For example, the metric system has base units of meters, liters, and grams. Meters measure length, liters measure volume, and grams measure mass. The metric system is convenient in math and science because it follows the base-ten number system. This means that quick calculations and conversions can be done simply by multiplying or dividing by a power of ten. For example, 10 millimeters is equivalent to 1 centimeter.

The customary system has much more than three units. For example, when measuring volume, options include ounces, cups, pints, quarts, and gallons. Converting between units is more challenging because each unit has a different conversion factor. For example, there are 4 quarts in a gallon, but 16 ounces in a pint. Distance is measured in inches, feet, yards, and miles. Mass is similar to weight, and is measured in ounces, pounds, and tons. It is important to become familiar with units in the metric and customary systems.

Customary Units

- **1 ounce**: about the weight of a candy bar
- **1 pound**: about the weight of a football
- **1 ton**: about the weight of a car

- **1 inch**: about the width of a quarter
- **1 foot**: about the height of a 2 liter soda bottle (12 inches)
- **1 yard**: about the width of a door (3 feet)
- **1 mile**: about 4 laps on an outdoor running track

- **1 ounce**: the amount of liquid in two tablespoons
- **1 cup**: the amount of liquid in a coffee cup (8 ounces)
- **1 pint**: the amount of liquid in a small water bottle (16 ounces)
- **1 quart**: the amount of liquid in a jug of juice (2 pints)
- **1 gallon**: the amount of liquid in a large container of milk

Metric Units

- **Meter:** about the width of a door frame
- **Liter:** about the volume of a large water bottle
- **Gram:** about the mass of a paperclip

Converting Between Units

Metric System

When converting units within the metric system, simply multiply or divide by a factor of 10. Notice the base unit is bolded (1 meter, 1 gram and 1 liter).

Length	Weight	Volume
1 km = 1,000 m	1 kg = 1,000 g	1 kL = 1,000 L
1 m = 0.001 km	1 g = 0.001 kg	1 L = 0.001 kL
1 m = 100 cm	**1 g** = 100 cg	**1 L** = 100 cL
1 cm = 0.01 m	1 cg = 0.01 g	1 cL = 0.01 L
1 m = 1,000 mm	1 g = 1,000 mg	1 L = 1,000 mL
1 mm = 0.001 m	1 mg = 0.001 g	1 mL = 0.001 L

For example, 2.56 meters is equivalent to 256 centimeters because meters are 100 times larger than centimeters. 3,366 millimeters is equivalent to 3.366 meters because millimeters are 1,000 times smaller than meters. Conversions in the metric system are quick because all it requires is knowing where to move the decimal point. Remember, each decimal movement to the right represents multiplication by 10. Each decimal movement to the left represents division by 10.

Review Video: Metric System Conversion
Visit mometrix.com/academy and enter code: 163709

Customary System

Converting within the customary system is more complicated. For this reason, the metric system is generally the system used in math and science. Notice how there is not really any pattern to follow when converting from one unit to the next. For example, there are 5,280 feet in a mile, but there are 12 inches in a foot.

Length	Weight	Volume
12 in = 1 ft	16 oz = 1 lb	128 fl. oz = 1 gal
3 ft = 1yd	2,000 lb = 1 ton	2 pt = 1 qt
5,280 ft = 1 mi		8 pt = 1 gal
1,760 yd = 1 mi		4 qt = 1 gal

Solving Problems Involving Measurements

When solving problems involving units for mass, length, or volume, first identify whether the units are metric or customary. Once this has been determined, think about how much you will need to multiply or divide by to make the **conversion**. For example, consider the following scenario.

James is pouring 4 gallons of juice into pints. How many pints can James pour if he pours out all the juice?

Ask yourself, "are these customary or metric units?" These are customary units.

Now, consider how many pints are in 4 gallons. There are 4 quarts in a gallon, so there are 16 quarts total.

There are 8 pints in a quart, so there are 16×8 total pints.

$$16 \times 8 = 128$$

James can pour 128 pints of juice.

Example

A baseball game started at 7:10. The game ended at 9:15. How long did the game last?

Count up by hours and then count up by minutes. 7:10 to 8:10 is one hour. 8:10 to 9:10 is one hour. 9:10 to 9:15 is 5 minutes. Altogether, this is 2 hours and 5 minutes.

Example

A tablet weighs 265 grams. Does a stack of 8 of these tablets have a mass that is more or less than 1 kilogram? (1 kg = 1,000 g)

Each tablet has a mass of 265 grams, so 8 tablets have a mass of 8×265 g = 2,120 kg. The mass of 8 tablets is 2,120 grams. 1 kilogram consists of 1,000 grams. 2,120 > 1,000, so the tablets have a mass greater than 1 kilogram.

Solving Using the Area and Perimeter of Rectangles

The **area** of a rectangle is calculated by multiplying the **length** and the **width**. For example, the rectangle below has a length of 8 yards and a width of 3 yards. So, the area of the rectangle is $8 \times 3 = 24$ square yards.

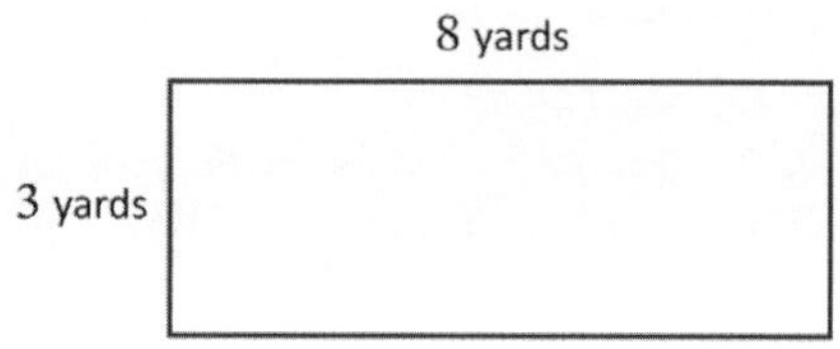

The **perimeter** of a rectangle is calculated by adding all four **side lengths**.

$$\text{Perimeter} = \text{length} + \text{length} + \text{width} + \text{width}$$

Another way to calculate perimeter: $P = 2l + 2w$.

A rectangle has 2 lengths and 2 widths, and the sum of these 4 sides is the perimeter. For example, the rectangle below has a length of 32 meters and a width of 20 meters.

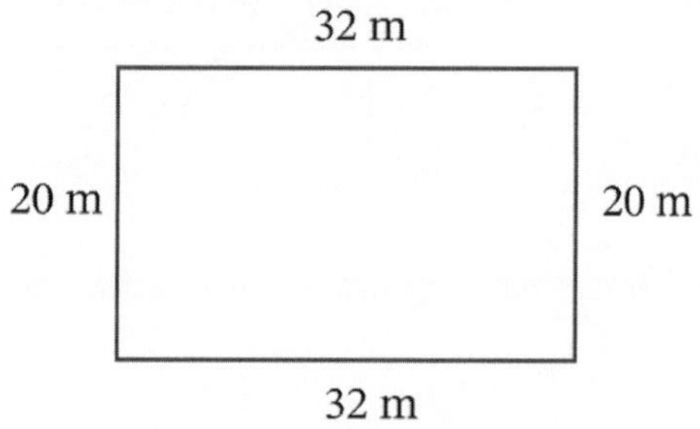

$$P = 32 + 32 + 20 + 20$$

$$P = (2 \times 32) + (2 \times 20)$$

Both equations simplify to 104, so the perimeter of the rectangle is 104 meters.

Variation in Rectangle Construction

A group of rectangles can have the same area but different perimeters. For example, consider a rectangle with an area of 20 square feet. How can this rectangle be built?

The rectangle may have a length of 1 foot and a width of 20 feet.

The rectangle may have a length of 2 feet and a width of 10 feet.

The rectangle may have a length of 4 feet and a width of 5 feet.

All three of these rectangles have an area of 20 square feet. However, each rectangle has a unique perimeter.

1 foot by 20 feet: Perimeter of 42 feet.

2 feet by 10 feet: Perimeter of 24 feet.

4 feet by 5 feet: Perimeter of 18 feet.

Now, consider a rectangle with a perimeter of 10 meters. There is more than one correct way to build this rectangle. For example, a 3-meter by 2-meter rectangle has a perimeter of 10 meters and an area of 6 square meters. However, a 4-meter by 1-meter rectangle also has a perimeter of 10 meters but it has an area of 4 square meters.

Review Video: Area and Perimeter of Rectangles and Squares
Visit mometrix.com/academy and enter code: 428109

Example

A city planner is creating a model design for new green space. The model has an area of 96 square centimeters and a length of 12 centimeters. What is the width of the model?

The area of a rectangle is calculated by multiplying the length by the width: $A = l \times w$. In this scenario, the area and the length are provided. Substitute A and l into the formula.

$$A = l \times w$$

$$96 = 12 \times w$$

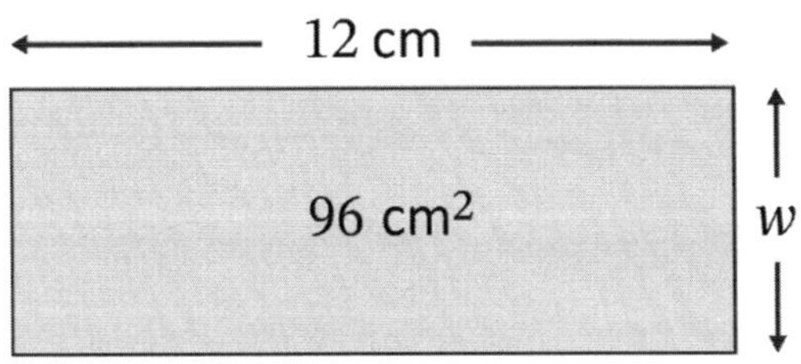

Divide 96 by 12 to find the width.

$$w = 96 \div 12 = 8$$

The width of the model is 8 centimeters.

Example

Student A says there is only one way to draw a rectangle with a perimeter of 14 units. Student B says there is more than one way do draw a rectangle with a perimeter of 14 units. Which student is correct? Support your answer with a model.

Option 1: 2 by 5. This rectangle has an area of 10 square units and a perimeter of 14 units.

Option 2: 1 by 6. This rectangle has an area of 6 square units and a perimeter of 14 units.

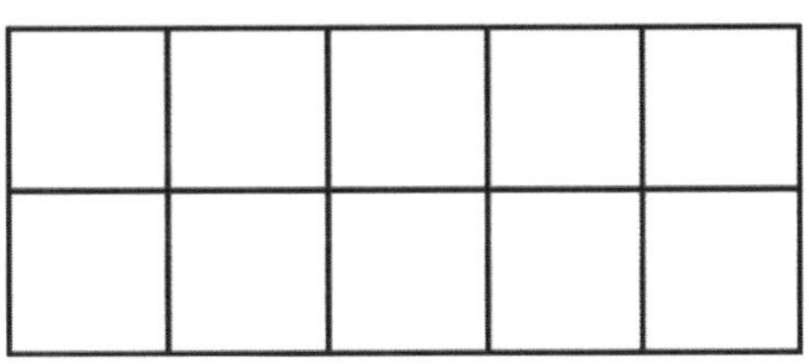

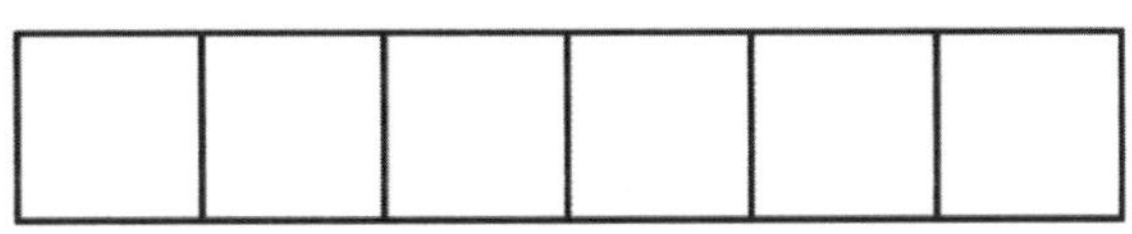

Student B is correct. There is more than one way to draw a rectangle with a perimeter of 14 units.

Representing Data

Data comes from a collection of facts or information. **Data** can be collected by observing, questioning, or measuring. It is common for data to be displayed using a **chart**, **table**, or **graph**. Three commonly used displays are frequency tables, dot plots, and stem-and-leaf plots. These displays can consist of whole number values or fractional values.

Dot Plot

A **dot plot** is a graph that uses dots above a number line to show the frequency of data. For example, the dot plot on the left shows how many books were read last summer by different students. The number of dots corresponds to the number of books each student read. 4 students read 0 books, 6 students read 1 book, and so on. The dot plot on the right shows the number of cups of different ingredients used in a pancake recipe. This dot plot shows that there is a total of $2\frac{5}{6}$ cups of ingredients needed for this recipe.

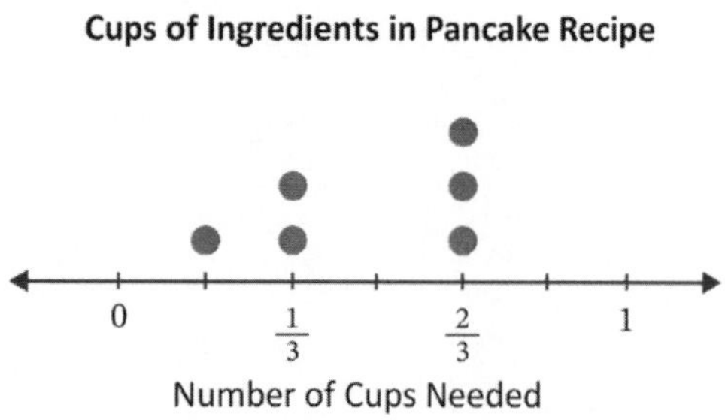

Frequency Table

Frequency tables are similar to dot plots because they show how often a data point occurs. Frequency tables list each value that appears in a data set, followed by the number of times it appears. Many frequency tables also include tally marks.

Favorite Subject	Tally Marks	Number of Students
Art	IIII	4
Mathematics	卌 II	7
Science	卌	5
English	IIII	4

Stem-and-Leaf Plot

Stem-and-leaf plots also display frequency. A **stem-and-leaf plot** splits numbers into separate digits based on place value. Larger place value digits are named stems and smaller place value digits are named leaves. For example, the stem-and-leaf plot below shows the tens digits on the left and the ones digits on the right. The first number represented is 41. The next three numbers represented are 52, 57, and 58. The digits are all listed in ascending order.

4	1
5	2 7 8
6	5 6
7	0 5 8 8 8
8	0 0
9	5

Key: 4|1 = 41

Solving Problems Involving Data Displays

Real-world problems can be solved by analyzing displays such as dot plots, frequency tables, and stem-and-leaf plots.

Number of Students in the Classrooms

Stems (tens)	Leaves (ones)
0	5 8
1	0 5 7
2	
3	1 1 2

Ways Children Get to School

Method of Traveling	Number of Children
Walking	8
Car	9
Bus	4
Cycle	5
Train	1
Taxi	3

Number of Books Checked Out from the Library

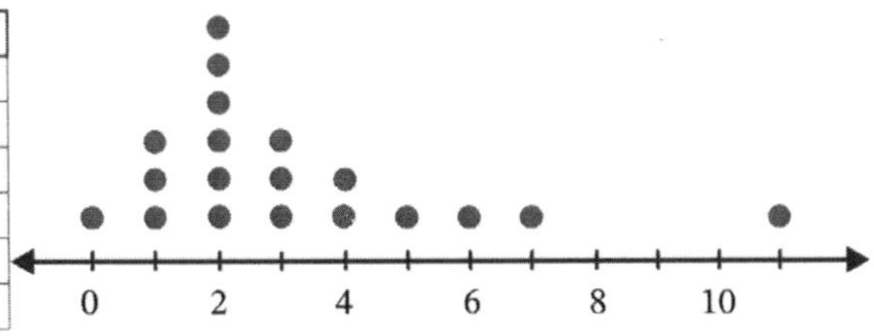

For example, which display shows values ranging from a minimum of 0 to a maximum of 11? The correct answer is the dot plot. This means one person checked out 0 books from the library and one person checked out 11 books from the library.

Which display has a maximum value of 9? The answer is the frequency table. There are 9 data points for the category "Car". This means that the most common way students get to school is by car.

Which display has two data points with a value of 31? The correct answer is the stem-and-leaf plot. This means that two classrooms have 31 students in them.

Many times, tests will ask you to identify information and then do something with it. For example, what is the difference between the number of children who walk to school and the number of children who ride the train to school?

First, we need to identify how many children walk to school. According to the frequency table, 8 children walk to school. We can also see that 1 child rides the train to school. After identifying the needed information, we can use it to answer the question. Since the question asks for the difference, we need to subtract 1 from 8: $8 - 1 = 7$. Therefore, the difference between the number of children who walk to school and the number of children who ride the train to school is 7.

These displays can be used to represent real-world scenarios. Dot plots, frequency tables, and stem-and-leaf plots are great for showing frequency in a way that is organized and structured.

Review Video: Stem and Leaf Plots
Visit mometrix.com/academy and enter code: 302339

EXAMPLE

A group of athletes are recording the number of miles they run each month. The stem-and-leaf plot shows the number of miles that each member of the group has run so far this month. What is the difference between the lowest mileage and the highest mileage?

Stem	Leaf
1	0 0 5 5 5
2	
3	7
4	
5	
6	5
7	0 0
8	6 8

The lowest mileage is 10 miles. The highest mileage is 88 miles. Subtract to find the difference: $88 - 10 = 78$. The difference in the lowest mileage and highest mileage is 78 miles.

EXAMPLE

A group of students have started a book club. The display below shows the progress each student has made reading the assigned book. Each X represents 1 student. How many students have read more than half of the book? How many students have read exactly half of the book so far?

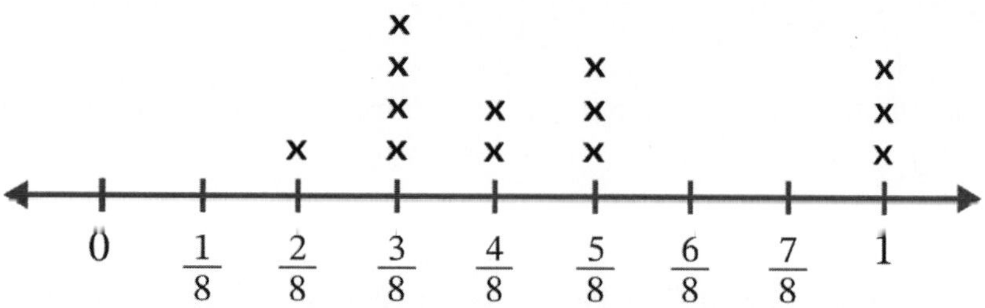

Each X represents 1 student. $\frac{4}{8}$ represents half of the book, and there are 2 Xs on $\frac{4}{8}$. This means 2 students have read exactly half of the book. There are 3 Xs on $\frac{5}{8}$ and 3 Xs on 1. This means that 6 students have read more than half of the book.

Comparing Data

To compare data, we need to understand measures of center, the spread of data distribution, the shape of data, and how to interpret data from dot plots and box plots.

Measures of Center

The **measures of center** are different methods for estimating or measuring the center of a data set. The center of a data set can be described by the most frequent value in a data set, the value appearing in the middle of a data set arranged from least to greatest, or the value that is the average of that data set. The terms used to describe the center of a data set are mode, median, and mean.

Mode

The **mode** of a data set is the number that shows up most frequently.

Let's say we are given this data set.

$$\{0, 0, 1, 1, 1, 1, 1, 1, 1, 1, 1, 1, 2, 2, 2, 2, 3, 4, 5\}$$

The mode in a data set is the number that repeats the most frequently. If we look at this list of values, we can see that 1 shows up the most often, so the mode of this data set is 1.

Median

The **median** of a data set is the literal middle value in a set of values. If you have a list of values, the median is going to be the value directly in the middle of a list of these values when the values are listed from least to greatest.

Let's say we have a set of data in a list.

$$\{3, 2, 2, 3, 0, 1, 2, 1, 1, 6, 2, 4, 2, 3, 6, 0, 0, 1, 1, 2, 4, 2, 4, 3, 1\}$$

This is a list of values, and we can determine the center, or median value in the data set by lining the values up from least to greatest and finding the middle value.

$$\{0, 0, 0, 1, 1, 1, 1, 1, 1, 2, 2, 2, 2, 2, 2, 2, 3, 3, 3, 3, 4, 4, 4, 6, 6\}$$

Now that we have our data set listed from least to greatest, the median will be the middle number in the set.

12 — 12

0 0 0 1 1 1 1 1 1 2 2 2 (2) 2 2 2 3 3 3 3 4 4 4 6 6

The center, or median value in this data set is 2, because when you list the values from least to greatest, 2 is the middle number. It is in the middle because it is the same distance from the smallest value to the greatest value and there are the same number of values, 12, on each side.

Finding the median of a data set that has even number of values requires a slightly different approach.

Let's say we are given this data set.

$$\{15, 16, 18, 20, 22, 12, 13, 14, 19, 21, 21, 11, 12, 14\}$$

First, we need to list the values from least to greatest to find the middle.

$$\{11, 12, 12, 13, 14, 14, 15, 16, 18, 19, 20, 21, 21, 22\}$$

Now, we can count to find the middle.

11 12 12 13 14 14 15|16 18 19 20 21 21 22

In this data set, there is not a middle number. Instead, the middle position lies between 15 and 16. So, to find the median value, we will have to find the mean of the two middle numbers, 15 and 16.

To find the mean of these middle values, we will add them together and divide by 2.

$$15 + 16 = 31$$
$$31 \div 2 = 15.5$$

So, the median of this data set is 15.5.

MEAN

The **mean** of a data set is often called the **average**. To find the mean of a data set, add the values in the data set together, and divide the sum by the total number of values.

In school, we are familiar with the mean of data sets because this is the way average grades are calculated. To get a final grade, often teachers will add the grade on each assignment or test together and divide by the total number of assignments or tests.

Let's say you are in a math class and your scores are listed in a data set.

$$\{76, 82, 82, 84, 87, 90, 85, 100, 94, 90\}$$

To find the mean, or average, of your scores, add the values and divide by the number of values. In this data set, if we add all the given grades together, we will get a total of 870. Now, if we divide 870 by the total number of grades, 10, we will get 87. That means that the final grade, the average grade, or the mean of the data set is 87.

Review Video: Mean, Median, and Mode
Visit mometrix.com/academy and enter code: 286207

EXAMPLE

The graph shows the number of students in each 6th grade homeroom class.

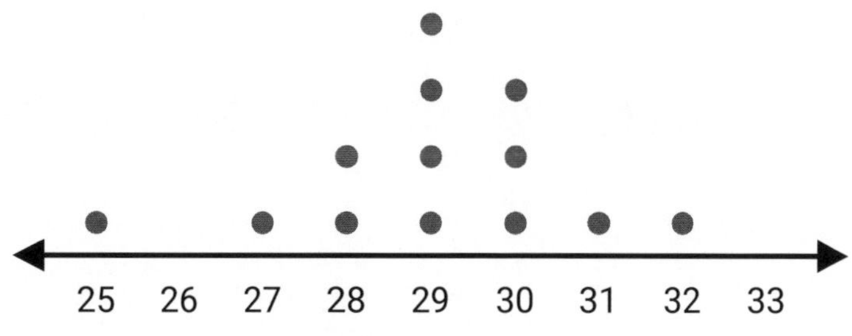

What is the mean number of students in each 6th grade homeroom class?

In this problem, we are given a dot plot that shows the number of students in each 6th grade homeroom class. We need to find the mean number of students in each class.

The mean is the average, and this is found by adding all values and dividing by the number of values.

To approach this problem, we need to start by decoding the graph. Let's list the values on the graph. The order that we write the values does not matter, but let's order them from least to greatest.

$$25, 27, 28, 28, 29, 29, 29, 29, 30, 30, 30, 31, 32$$

There are a total of 13 dots, so there are 13 homeroom classes. Now we need to add the number of students in all 13 classes.

$$25 + 27 + 28 + 28 + 29 + 29 + 29 + 29 + 30 + 30 + 30 + 31 + 32 = 377$$

So, there are 377 6th grade students. Now, to find the mean, we need to take the total value and divide by the number of values. In other words, divide the number of students by the number of classes.

There are 13 classes, or 13 values, so we need to divide 377 by 13.

377 divided by 13 is 29, so the mean number of students in each class is 29.

EXAMPLE

The table shows the amount of rainfall each day in inches during the rainiest 2 weeks in April.

Rainfall April 1-14

April 1-7	4.0 in	1.2 in	3.5 in	3.8 in	0.0 in	2.4 in	0.0 in
April 8-14	3.1 in	3.5 in	3.4 in	1.0 in	4.5 in	6.0 in	0.2 in

What is the median amount of daily rainfall during these weeks?

In this problem, we are given a table showing the rainfall over 14 days and need to find the median amount of daily rainfall during this time.

The median value is the middle value in a data set. To approach this problem, we need to start by listing the values from least to greatest.

$$0.0, 0.0, 0.2, 1.0, 1.2, 2.4, 3.1, 3.4, 3.5, 3.5, 3.8, 4.0, 4.5, 6.0$$

Now that the values are listed from least to greatest, we can find the middle of the data set.

$$0.0\ 0.0\ 0.2\ 1.0\ 1.2\ 2.4\ 3.1 | 3.4\ 3.5\ 3.5\ 3.8\ 4.0\ 4.5\ 6.0$$

The middle of this data set falls in the middle of two numbers. So, to find the median amount of rainfall, we need to find the mean of these two middle values, 3.1 inches and 3.4 inches. To find the mean of these amounts, we need to add the two values and divide by 2.

$$3.1 + 3.4 = 6.5$$
$$6.5 \div 2 = 3.25$$

The median amount of rainfall during these two weeks is 3.25 inches.

Spread of a Data Distribution

The **spread** of a data distribution is a way to describe the range, or how spread out or close together the data is. Data with a large spread means that there is a large variety of values, or the values are far away from each other. Data with a small spread means that there is not very much variety of values, or the values are close to each other. There are two ways we describe the spread of data. One way to describe the spread is through **range**. The range of data is the difference between the smallest value and the largest value.

Let's say you are given two sets of data.

Data Set 1

953	1,634	1,348	450	2,349	879
1,334	2,145	587	994	1,045	950
2,231	1,287	1,898	1,934	2,150	2,476

Data Set 2

3	6	1
2	3	2
2	0	7
4	4	3
5	2	3

Let's compare the range of these data sets. To compare the ranges, we need to identify the difference between smallest and largest values in each data set.

In data set 1, the smallest value is 450 and the largest value is 2,476. The rage in this data set is the difference between these two values, so we will use subtraction to identify the range.

$$2{,}476 - 450 = 2{,}026$$

So, the range of data set 1 is 2,026.

In data set 2, the smallest value is 0 and the largest value is 7. So, the range is the difference between these values.

$$7 - 0 = 7$$

So, the range of data set 2 is 7.

Now, we can compare. Data set 1 has a large range compared to data set 2 because 2,026 is greater than 7.

Time

Draw the time 7:20 on an analog clock and a digital clock.

On the analog clock, the small hand will be just after the 7, showing it is just after 7 o'clock. The big hand will be at 20 minutes, which is at 4.

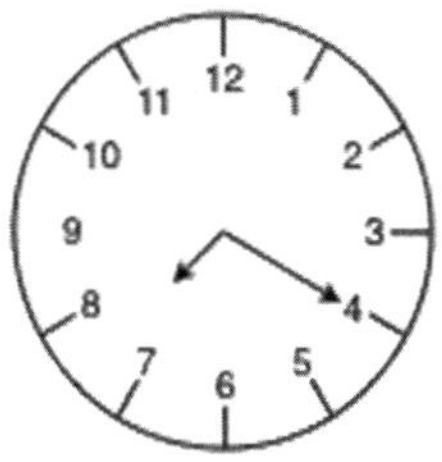

On a digital clock, the time will be written in the order: hours, then minutes. Since the hour is only one digit, there may be a 0 before the 7.

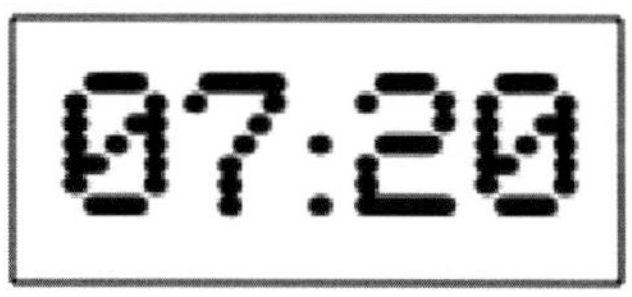

Find the time on the clock below.

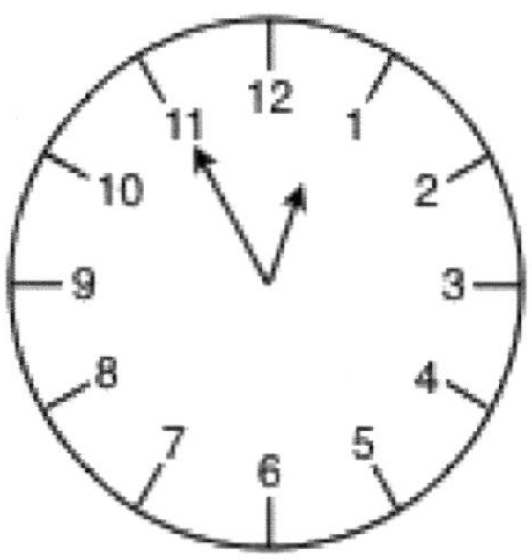

The big hand is on the 11, so the minutes is 55. The small hand is just before the 1, which means that it is close to 1 o'clock, but it is not yet 1 o'clock. It is still 12 o'clock. The time is 12:55.

Time Intervals

Things to Remember:

There are 60 seconds in 1 minute.
There are 60 minutes in 1 hour.
There are 24 hours in 1 day.
There are 365 days in 1 year.

Adding and Subtracting Time

When adding or subtracting time in minutes, an hour can be visualized as 4 sections of 15 minutes.

$\frac{1}{4}$ of an hour: 15 minutes

$\frac{2}{4}$ of an hour: 30 minutes

$\frac{3}{4}$ of an hour: 45 minutes

$\frac{4}{4}$ of an hour: 60 minutes

Strategies for Adding and Subtracting Time

For example, if a student practices the piano for 15 minutes a day, for 4 days, how long have they practiced in all?

Use a model. Each 15-minute session represents $\frac{1}{4}$ of an hour. $15 + 15 + 15 + 15 = 60$. So, the student has practiced for 60 minutes, which is 1 hour.

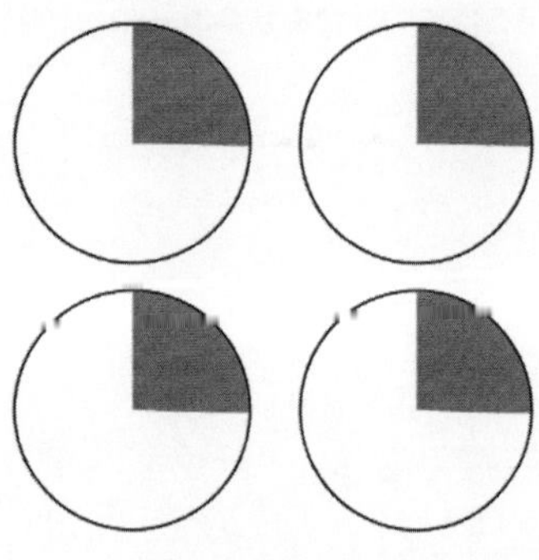

Using sections of the clock to add or subtract is a great way to solve problems mentally. Remember, one quarter of an hour is 15 minutes, and one half of an hour is 30 minutes. Skip counting by 15 or 30 is an efficient way to solve problems involving elapsed time. This also works for subtraction problems.

Consider the following scenario: A student studied 45 minutes for a math test, and 15 minutes for a science test. How much longer did the student study for the math test than the science test?

Math: 45 minutes
Science: 15 minutes

Subtract the time between studying for math and studying for science: $45 - 15 = 30$. This represents half an hour. The student spent 30 minutes more studying for the math test than the science test.

Practice Test #1

1. Andrea pays $120.76 more in rent per month this year than she did last year. She pays $763.48 per month this year. How much did she pay per month last year?

a. $643.72
b. $642.72
c. $643.32
d. $642.32

2. Which fraction is equivalent to the diagram shown below?

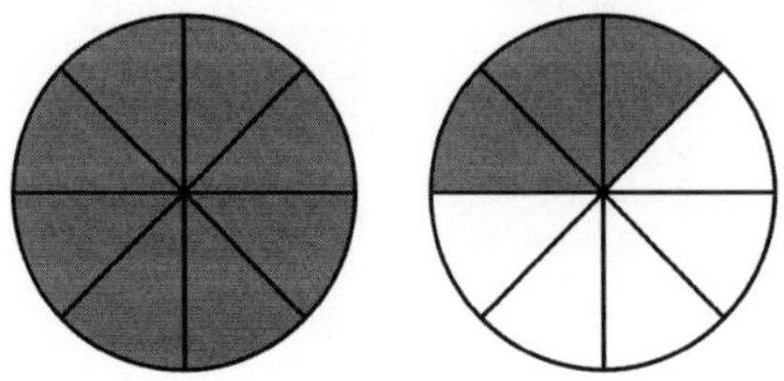

a. $1\frac{1}{8}$
b. $1\frac{1}{4}$
c. $1\frac{3}{8}$
d. $1\frac{1}{2}$

3. Which of the following models represents a fraction equivalent to $\frac{2}{5}$?

a.

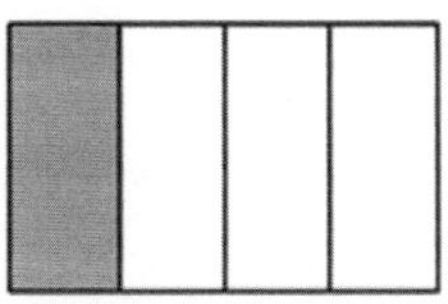

b.

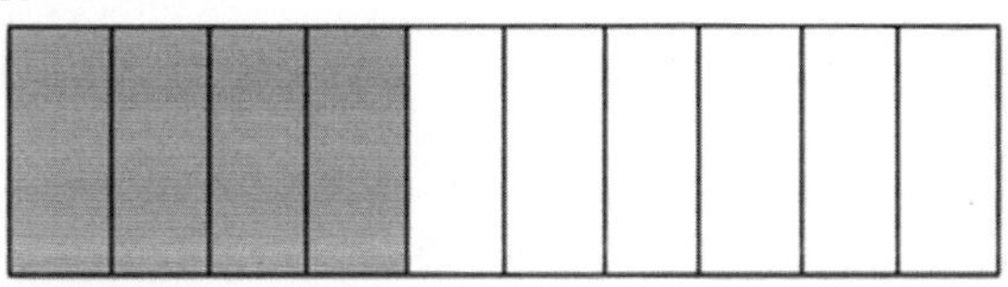

c.

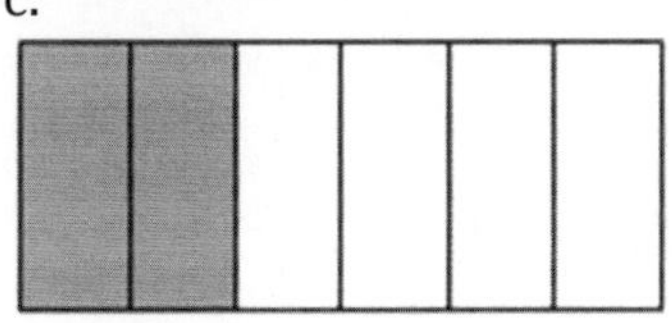

d.

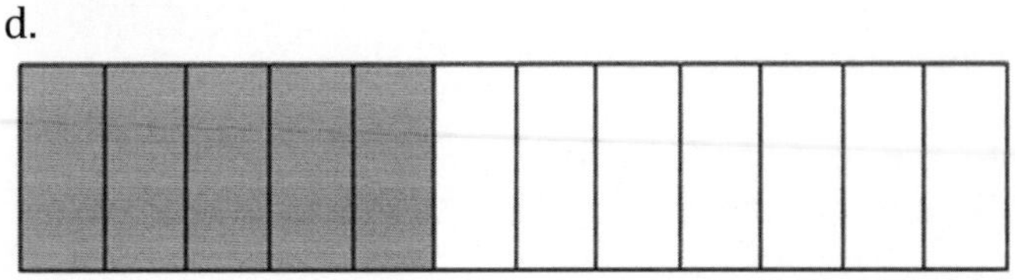

4. If Hannah drives 1104.02 miles a month and Carrie drives 1339.6 miles a month. How many miles do they drive each month combined?

a. 2,443.08
b. 2,444.62
c. 2,443.62
d. 2,443.8

5. Carly has two dogs. She purchases dog food in bags that contain 45 cups per bag. Each dog receives 5 cups of food each day. How many days can Carly feed her dogs if she purchases 8 bags?

a. 36 days
b. 30 days
c. 5 days
d. 20 days

6. Which of the following models represents a fraction less than the fraction shown below?

a.

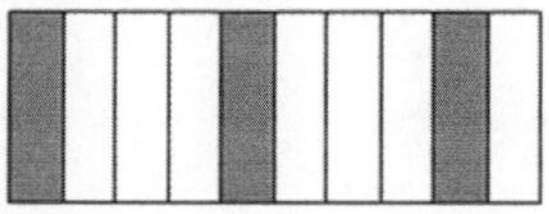

b.

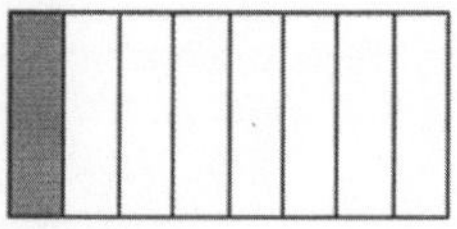

c.

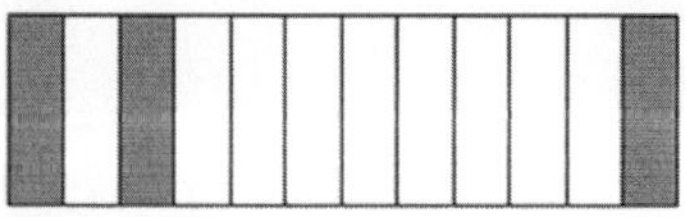

d.

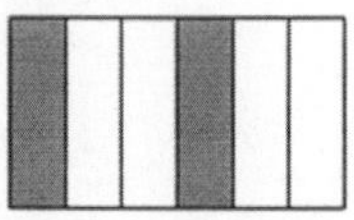

7. Amanda creates the base of a picture frame, using 4.55 inches of red fabric and 6.25 inches of blue fabric. How many inches of fabric are used to create the base of the frame?

a. 10.80 inches
b. 10.85 inches
c. 10.75 inches
d. 10.90 inches

8. Travis has a stick that is 5/16 of a meter long, and Steven has a stick that is 14/16 of a meter long. If they lay the sticks end to end how long would they be?

a. $\frac{12}{16}$
b. $1\frac{3}{16}$
c. $1\frac{3}{8}$
d. $1\frac{1}{8}$

9. 194 becomes ___ when rounded to the nearest ten. Write your answer in the blank below.

10. The list below shows the temperature in Fahrenheit in Alaska for seven days.

45°, 40°, 39°, 44°, 51°, 41°, 50°

Which frequency table correctly displays the data?

a.

	Temperature in Fahrenheit	Number of Days
Row 1	20° to 30°	I
Row 2	31° to 41°	II
Row 3	42° to 52°	III
Row 4	53° to 63°	I

b.

	Temperature in Fahrenheit	Number of Days
Row 1	20° to 30°	II
Row 2	31° to 41°	II
Row 3	42° to 52°	III
Row 4	53° to 63°	

c.

	Temperature in Fahrenheit	Number of Days
Row 1	20° to 30°	
Row 2	31° to 41°	III
Row 3	42° to 52°	IIII
Row 4	53° to 63°	

d.

	Temperature in Fahrenheit	Number of Days
Row 1	20° to 30°	
Row 2	31° to 41°	III
Row 3	42° to 52°	II
Row 4	53° to 63°	II

11. Hannah ran 12 laps every day for 8 days. How many laps did she run in all?

a. 108
b. 96
c. 84
d. 72

12. Kevin approved 13 trees out of every group of trees he surveyed. He surveyed 15 groups of trees. How many trees did he approve?

a. 155
b. 165
c. 195
d. 205

13. Monique has $690 to spend on a 3-day trip. She plans to spend an equal amount of money per day. How many dollars can she spend per day? Write your answer in the blank below.

14. Find the product of 34×28.

a. 951
b. 952
c. 953
d. 954

15. Lynn has $316 to spend on groceries for the month. He plans to spend the same amount of money on groceries each week. Which of the following is the best estimate for the amount of money he can spend on groceries each week?

a. $65
b. $75
c. $90
d. $95

16. Carlisle charges $21.95 per haircut and has completed 30 haircuts this week. Which of the following is the best approximation for the total charges for all haircuts?

a. $450
b. $600
c. $750
d. $800

17. Which of the following number sentences belongs in the fact family shown below?

$$7 \times 6 = 42$$
$$6 \times 7 = 42$$
$$42 \div 7 = 6$$

a. $7 + 6 = 13$
b. $42 \div 6 = 7$
c. $42 + 7 = 49$
d. $42 - 6 = 36$

18. Use the models to find the difference between the two fractions.

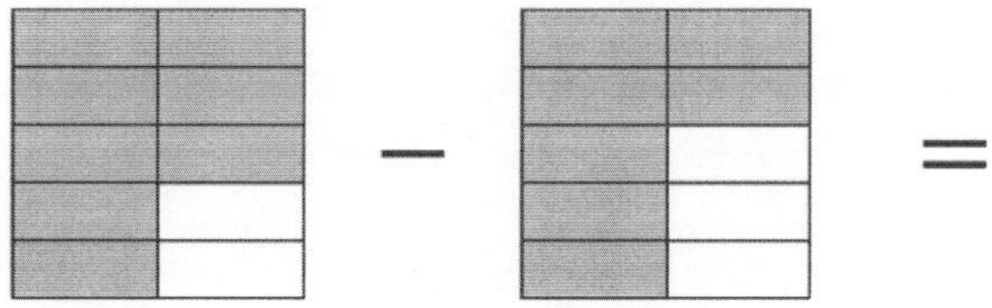

Which model below shows the difference between the two fractions represented above.

a.

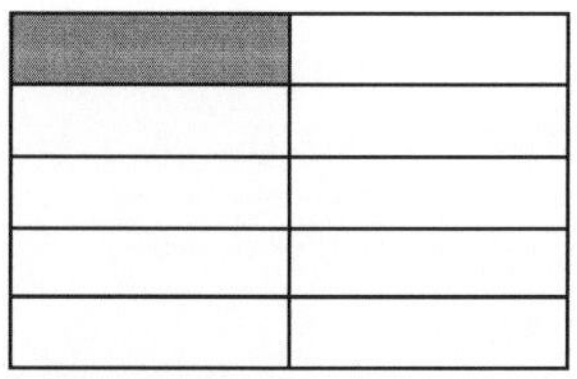

b.

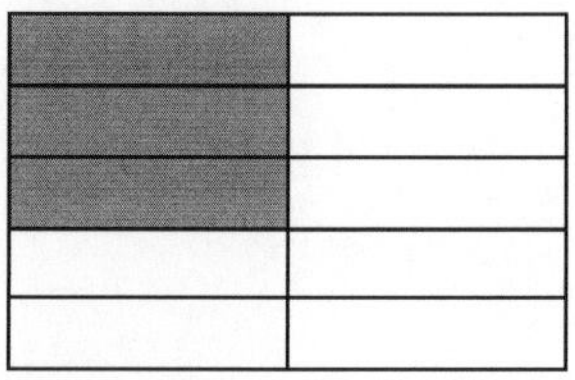

c.

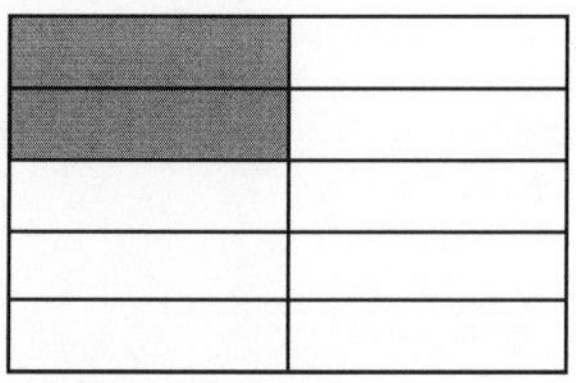

d.

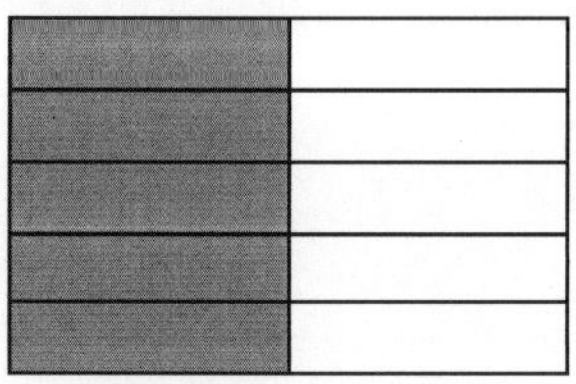

19. A door is $7\frac{1}{4}$ feet tall. How many inches is it? Write your answer in the blank below.

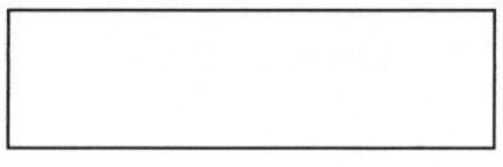

20. Mrs. Thompson writes the number sentences shown below:

$$100 \times 13 = 1300$$
$$100 \times 14 = 1400$$
$$100 \times 15 = 1500$$
$$100 \times 24 = ?$$

What is the product of the last number sentence?

a. 2200
b. 2300
c. 2400
d. 2500

21. The number of sit-ups Aisha has completed over a period of 3 days is shown in the table below.

Day	Number of Sit-ups
1	35
2	70
3	105

If this pattern continues, how many sit-ups will she have completed after 7 days? Write your answer in the blank below.

22. Use the model to find the sum of the two fractions.

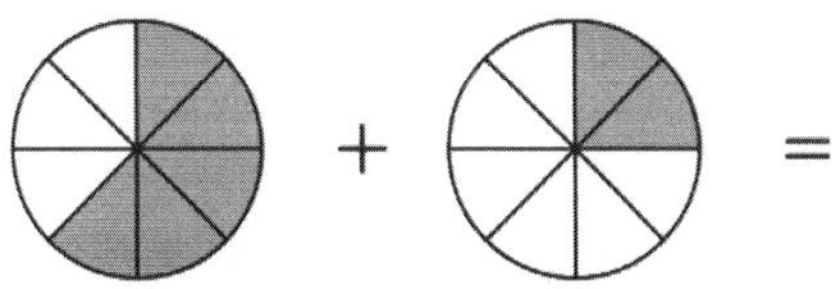

a. $\frac{8}{7}$
b. $\frac{10}{12}$
c. $\frac{7}{8}$
d. $\frac{7}{16}$

23. If the measure of angle *BAC* is 38° and the measure of angle *DAE* is 49°, then what is the measure of angle *CAD*? Write your answer in the blank below.

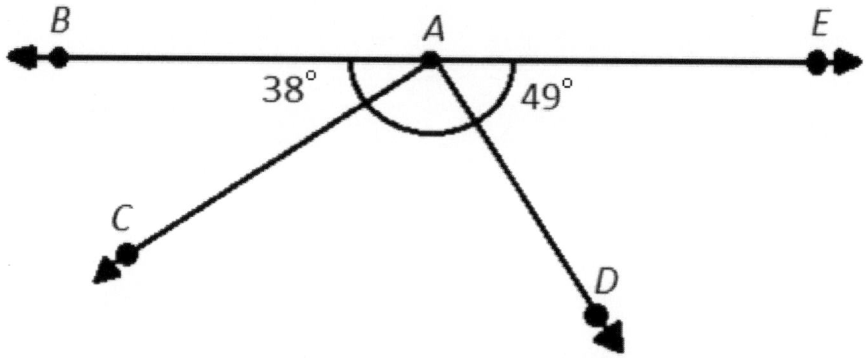

24. The area of a rectangle is 36 square inches. If the width of the rectangle is 4 inches, then what is its length?

a. 9 inches
b. 12 inches
c. 18 inches
d. 32 inches

25. The measure of the angle to the nearest degree is ___. Write your answer in the blank below.

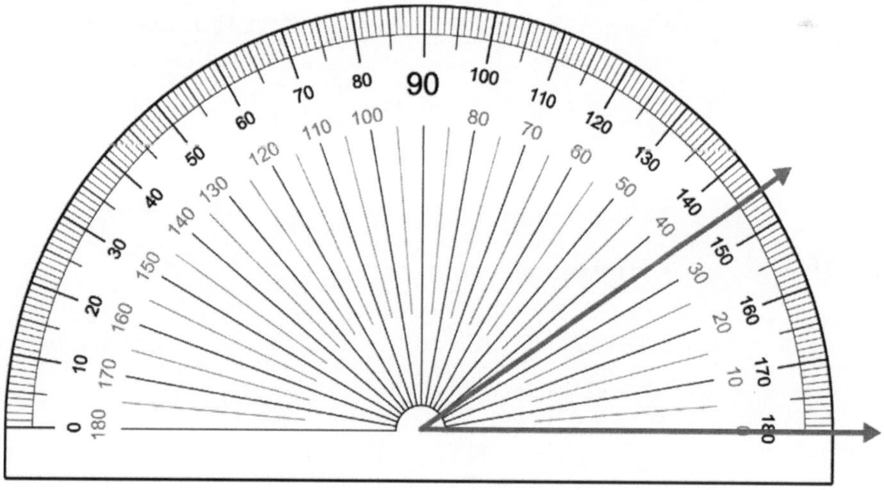

26. Given the numbers below, fill in the blank with the correct symbol (<, >, =) to make the statement true.

4.22 ____ 4.2

.09 ____ .9

2.72____ 2.702

27. Which of the following equation equals $4 \times \frac{4}{5}$?

a. $8 \times \frac{1}{5}$
b. $4 \times \frac{3}{5}$
c. $5 \times \frac{4}{5}$
d. $16 \times \frac{1}{5}$

28. Express the fraction $\frac{9}{100}$ as a decimal.

a. 0.9
b. 9.0
c. 0.09
d. 9.09

29. Amy makes custom dog collars out of leather. A small dog collar has a length of 8 inches and a width of 1 inch. A medium dog collar has a length of 9 inches and a width of 2 inches. A large dog collar has a length of 12 inches and a width of 2 inch. Amy needs to create 2 medium collars and 3 large collars. What is the area of leather that needs to be cut?

a. 108 square inches
b. 116 square inches
c. 120 square inches
d. 144 square inches

30. Which pair of fractions are equivalent?

a. $\frac{3}{4}$ and $\frac{6}{8}$
b. $\frac{3}{4}$ and $\frac{4}{8}$
c. $\frac{1}{4}$ and $\frac{1}{8}$
d. $\frac{3}{6}$ and $\frac{6}{8}$

31. The table shows numbers of meters and the equivalent numbers of centimeters. Julia has three pine trees in her backyard. One is 5 meters tall, one is 7 meters tall, and one is 10 meters tall. From the options below, write the height of each tree in centimeters in the table.

350	500	600	700	750	1,000

Meters	Centimeters
1	100
2	200
3	300
5	
7	
10	

32. Jason walks 2,847 feet to school. Kevin walks 3,128 feet to school. What is the difference in the distance that they walk to school? Write your answer in the blank below.

33. Ana draws a line with chalk that is $14\frac{5}{8}$ feet long. Then she erases $3\frac{3}{8}$ feet. How long is the line now? Write your answer in the blank below.

34. What is the range of the values listed in the stem and leaf plot?

Stem	Leaf
6	8
7	5 7 9
8	0 2
9	2 6 6 7

Key: 6|8 = 68

a. 802
b. 29
c. 96
d. 92,599

35. The measure of the angle to the nearest degree is ___. Write your answer in the blank below.

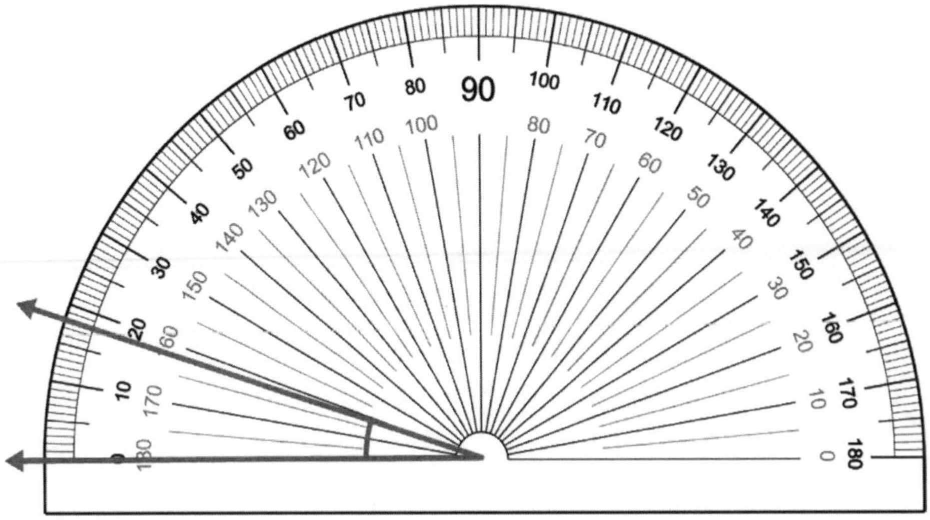

36. Sally is making cupcakes. She needs $\frac{1}{4}$ cup of sugar for every 3 cupcakes. How many cups does she need for 24 cupcakes?

a. $1\frac{1}{2}$ cups
b. 8 cups
c. $\frac{3}{4}$ cup
d. 2 cups

37. Aubrey arrived at the party at the time shown on the clock below. It is now four-thirty. How much time has passed since she arrived at the party?

2:15

a. 1 hour, 45 minutes
b. 2 hours, 5 minutes
c. 2 hours, 15 minutes
d. 2 hours, 30 minutes

38. Choose from the options below and write the correct answers in the blanks.

How many of the triangles below are considered right triangles?

___ of these triangles are considered right triangles because they each have ________________.

2	a right angle
3	three equal sides
4	an acute angle

39. An artist paints two canvases with the same area. One canvas is 2 feet by 8 feet, and the other canvas is 4 feet by 4 feet. The difference in the perimeter of the two canvases is ___ feet. Write your answer in the blank below.

40. The dot plot shows how many minutes students spent studying multiplication flash cards each day. Each dot represents 1 student. What is the mode of the data?

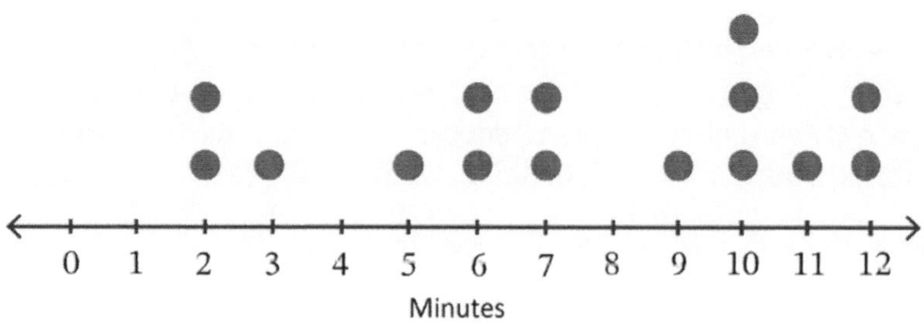

a. 12
b. 10
c. 3
d. 7

Answers and Explanations for Test #1

1. B: Since Andrea paid \$120.76 per month more this year, the amount she paid per month last year is equal to the difference of \$763.48 and \$120.76, or \$642.72.

$$\begin{array}{rcccccc} & & & 2 & & & \\ & 7 & 6 & \not{3} & . & \not{4} & 8 \\ - & 1 & 2 & 0 & . & 7 & 6 \\ \hline & 6 & 4 & 2 & . & 7 & 2 \end{array}$$

2. C: The diagram represents one whole, plus three-eighths of a second whole. Therefore, the diagram represents the fraction, $1\frac{3}{8}$.

3. B: The fraction, $\frac{2}{5}$, is equivalent to the fraction, $\frac{4}{10}$. The numerator and denominator of the given fraction are both multiplied by 2 to obtain the model for $\frac{4}{10}$; the fractions are proportional.

4.C: To find their combined miles add them together. When adding decimal numbers, make sure to line up the decimal place. Add using standard methods.

$$\begin{array}{rccccccc} & & & 1 & & & & \\ & 1 & 1 & 0 & 4 & . & 0 & 2 \\ + & 1 & 3 & 3 & 9 & . & 6 & 0 \\ \hline & 2 & 4 & 4 & 3 & . & 6 & 2 \end{array}$$

5. A: If Carly purchases 8 bags, she has 45×8 cups of food, which is 360 cups. Each dog needs 5 cups of food each day, so Carly uses $5 + 5$ cups each day, or 10 cups each day. Divide the total number of cups, 360, by the number of cups needed each day, 10, to calculate the number of days the bags of food will last, $360 \div 10 = 36$. The 8 bags of food will feed Carly's dogs for 36 days.

6. B: The given model represents the fraction, $\frac{2}{9}$, which is approximately 0.22. The model for Choice B represents the fraction, $\frac{1}{8}$, which equals 0.125. This fraction is less than the given fraction. The fractions can also be compared by finding a least common denominator.

7. A: The sum of the two decimals is 10.80; the decimals are added just like whole numbers are, while aligning the decimal point.

8. B: If they lay the sticks end to end then you would just add the lengths together. Add $\frac{14}{16}$ to $\frac{5}{16}$ to get $\frac{19}{16}$. When adding fractions, the denominators have to be the same. Add the numerators together but keep the same denominator. Since the numerator is larger than the denominator, it is an improper fraction. Subtract one whole from the fraction to convert it to a mixed number. Since $\frac{19}{16} - \frac{16}{16} = \frac{3}{16}$, put the whole number in front of the remaining fraction which equals $1\frac{3}{16}$.

9. 190: Start by locating the number in the tens place. In the number 194, there is a 9 in the tens place. Now look to the number to the right. If the number to the right is 4 or less, 194 will become 190. If the number to the right is 5 or more, 194 will become 200. In this case, 4 is to the right of the tens place. This means 194 becomes 190 when rounded to the nearest ten.

10. C: Rows 2 and 3 are incomplete. Row 2 shows the frequency of temperatures ranging from 31° to 41°. Three temperatures fall into this range, so three tally marks are needed in Row 2. Row 3 shows the frequency of temperatures ranging from 42° to 52°. Four temperatures fall into this range, so four tally marks are needed in Row 3. All of the temperatures fall into these two ranges. This means that there should not be any tally marks in Row 1 or Row 4.

11. B: She runs 12×8 laps in all, or 96 laps.

12. C: Since he approved 13 trees out of every group of trees and surveyed 15 groups, he approved 13×15 trees, or 195 trees.

13. 230: In order to find the amount of money she can spend each day, 690 should be divided by 3; $690 \div 3 = 230$. Thus, she can spend 230 dollars per day.

14. B: One way to solve this problem is by using an area model. Create an area model with 4 empty squares. Write 34 as $30 + 4$, and write 28 as $20 + 8$. Multiply to fill in each square. Add all four values. The answer is 952.

$$34 \times 28$$

	20	8
30	600	240
4	80	32

$$\begin{array}{r} 32 \\ 80 \\ 240 \\ +\ 600 \\ \hline 952 \end{array}$$

15. B: The amount of money Lynn has to spend on groceries for the month can be rounded to \$300; $300 \div 4 = 75$. Thus, the best estimate for the amount of money he can spend per week is \$75.

16. B: The amount of money Carlisle charges per hair cut can be rounded to \$20; $20 \times 30 = 600$. Thus, his total charges are approximately \$600.

17. B: The missing number sentence in the fact family is the other division number sentence, which reads:$42 \div 6 = 7$.

18. A: Each picture shows 10 equal shares. This means each shaded share represents $\frac{1}{10}$. The model on the left shows 8 shaded shares, or $\frac{8}{10}$. The model on the right shows that 7 shares are subtracted. When 7 shares are subtracted from 8 shares, 1 share remains. $\frac{8}{10} - \frac{7}{10} = \frac{1}{10}$, so $\frac{1}{10}$ is the difference. The model has 10 shares, so one of the shares must be shaded to represent the fraction $\frac{1}{10}$.

19. 87 in.: There are 12 inches in a foot. $12 \times 7 = 84$. Then divide 12 by 4 to get 3. 84+3=87.

20. C: As noted in the pattern, the product of 100 and 24 can be found by multiplying 24 by 1 and adding two zeros to the product. Thus, the product of 100 and 24 is 2400.

21. 245. Since she completes 35 each day, she has completed 35×7 situps after 7 days; $35 \times 7 = 245$.

22. C: Each circle has 8 equal shares, so each share represents $\frac{1}{8}$. The circle on the left has 5 shaded shares. The circle on the left has 2 shaded shares. $5 + 2 = 7$, so 7 shares are shaded, and each share is $\frac{1}{8}$. This means $\frac{7}{8}$ are shaded: $\frac{5}{8} + \frac{2}{8} = \frac{7}{8}$.

23. 93°: Since the angle of a straight line is known to be 180°, then $38°$ *and* $49°$can be subtracted from that to get 93°.

24. A: The area of a rectangle is calculated by multiplying the length and the width, $A = l \times w$.

In this case, A and w are provided, but l is unknown.

$$36 = l \times 4$$

We find that $4 \times 9 = 36$, so the missing dimension is 9 inches.

25. 35: The right interior row of numbers starts at 0°. Start at 0° and move counterclockwise to meet the other ray. The other ray passes through 35° on the interior row of numbers, so the angle measures 35°.

26. 4.22 > 4.2

.09 < .9

2.72 > 2.702

27. D: To multiply a whole number by a fraction, multiply the whole number by the numerator only to receive the product. When multiplying 16 by 1/5th, multiply 16 by 1, and leave the denominator as 5. The product is 16/5. Similarly, when multiplying 4 by 4/5, the product is 16/5.

28. C: The fraction $\frac{9}{100}$ represents 9 hundredths. As a decimal, this means 9 in the hundredths place. The decimal 0.09 represents the fraction $\frac{9}{100}$.

29. A: A medium collar is 9 inches by 2 inches, so the area of one medium collar is $9 \times 2 = 18$ square inches. Amy needs two of these, which results in a total of $2 \times 18 = 36$ square inches. A large collar is 12 inches by 2 inches, so the area of one large collar is $12 \times 2 = 24$ square inches. Amy needs three of these, which results in a total of $3 \times 24 = 72$ square inches. Add the two totals together to get the amount of leather Amy needs to cut, $36 + 72 = 108$ square inches. Amy needs to cut 108 square inches of leather for the project.

30. A: $\frac{3}{4}$ and $\frac{6}{8}$ are equivalent because they are the same distance from 0 on a number line.

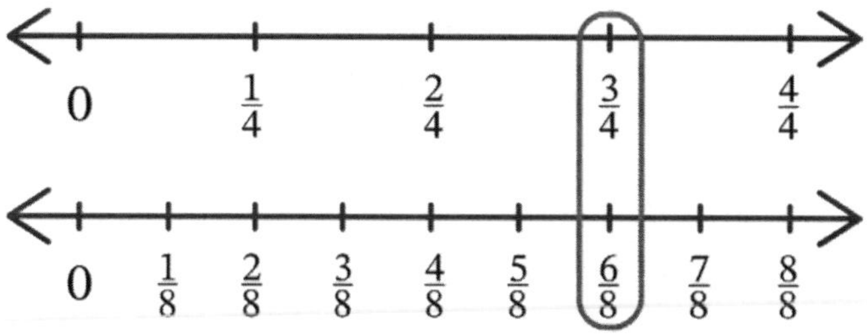

31. 500; 700; 1,000: There are 100 centimeters in every meter. The first pine tree is 5 meters tall, therefore it is $5 \times 100 = 500$ centimeters tall. The second pine tree is 7 meters tall, so it is $7 \times 100 = 700$ centimeters tall. The third pine tree is 10 meters tall, therefore, it is $10 \times 100 = 1{,}000$ centimeters tall.

32. 281: To find the difference just subtract. 3128-2847=281

33. $11\frac{1}{4}$: To find the length just subtract $3\frac{3}{8}$ from $14\frac{5}{8}$.

34. B: The stem and leaf plot shows the tens digit in the stem and the ones digit in the leaf. 9 in the stem and 7 in the leaf represents the value 97. This is the largest value in the stem and leaf plot. 6 in the stem and 8 in the leaf represents the value 68. This is the smallest value in the stem and leaf plot. To find the range of the values, subtract 68 from 97, which is equal to 29.

35. 18: The left exterior row of numbers starts at 0°. Start at 0° and move clockwise to meet the other ray. The other ray passes through 18° on the exterior row of numbers, so the angle measures 18°.

36. D: If she needs to make 24 cupcakes and she knows the amount of sugar for 3 cupcakes then she just needs to multiply by 8. So $\frac{1}{4} \times 8 = \frac{8}{4} = 2$.

37. C: From 2:15 to 4:15, two hours have passed. From 4:15 to 4:30, 15 additional minutes have passed. Therefore, the elapsed time is 2 hours, 15 minutes.

38. 2, a right angle: A right triangle contains a 90° angle. A 90° angle can be thought of as a corner angle. Two triangles in the group, the second and third triangles have 90° corner angles. The second and the third triangles are right triangles.

39. 4: The canvas that is 2 by 8 has a perimeter of 20 feet.

$$P = 2l + 2w$$

$$P = 2 \times 2 + 2 \times 8$$

$$P = 4 + 16$$

$$P = 20$$

The canvas that is 4 by 4 has a perimeter of 16 feet.

$$P = 2l + 2w$$

$$P = 2 \times 4 + 2 \times 4$$

$$P = 8 + 8$$

$$P = 16$$

The difference between 20 and 16 is 4.

$$20 - 16 = 4$$

The first canvas has a perimeter that is 4 feet more than the second canvas even though the areas are the same of both canvases.

40. B: The dot plot shows the frequency of students studying for certain amounts of time. The display shows 3 dots above 10 minutes, which means 3 students studied for 10 minutes. The mode of the data is the number that is repeated the most. Since 10 minutes is the only one that has three students, 10 is the mode since it occurs the most often.

Practice Test #2

1. A room has 6 rows of 9 chairs. The room next to it has 32 chairs. Together how many chairs do they have?

a. 54
b. 56
c. 86
d. 84

2. $\angle ADB$ has a measure of 42°. $\angle BDC$ has a measure of 64°. What is the measure in degrees of $\angle ADC$?

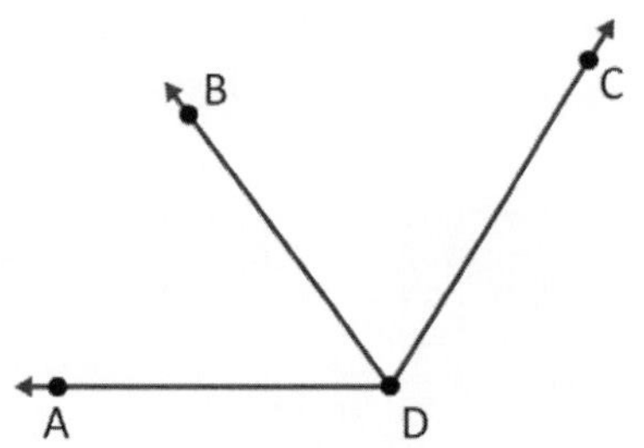

a. 106°
b. 116°
c. 96°
d. 126°

3. Which of the following sets represents a fraction equivalent to $\frac{8}{12}$?

a.

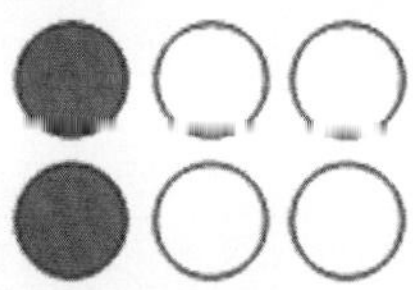

b.

c.

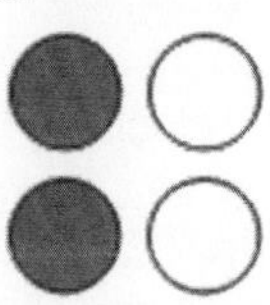

d.

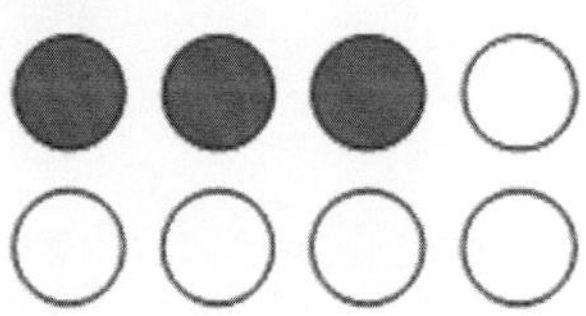

4. Which fraction is equivalent to the diagram shown below?

a. $1\frac{1}{2}$
b. $1\frac{2}{5}$
c. $1\frac{3}{5}$
d. $1\frac{3}{4}$

5. Which of the following models represents a fraction equal to the fraction shown below?

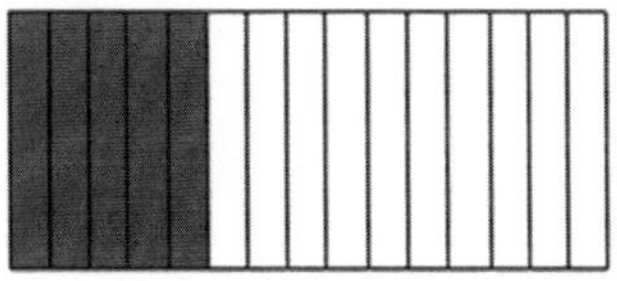

a.

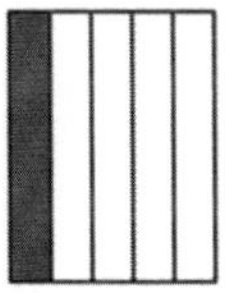

b.

c.

d.

6. Which of the following fractions are equal to $\frac{2}{3}$?

a. $\frac{1}{6}$
b. $\frac{6}{9}$
c. $\frac{5}{8}$
d. $\frac{6}{10}$

7. Martin saved $156.78 in September, $173.35 in October, and $219.65 in November. How much money did he save during the three months?

a. $438.68
b. $538.68
c. $549.78
d. $548.78

8. Peter put a tray of cookies in the oven at 4:35 P.M. He took the tray of cookies out of the oven 12 minutes later. What time did he take the cookies out of the oven?

a. 4:47 P.M.
b. 4:46 P.M.
c. 4:45 P.M.
d. 4:44 P.M.

9. Which sum is represented by the diagram shown below?

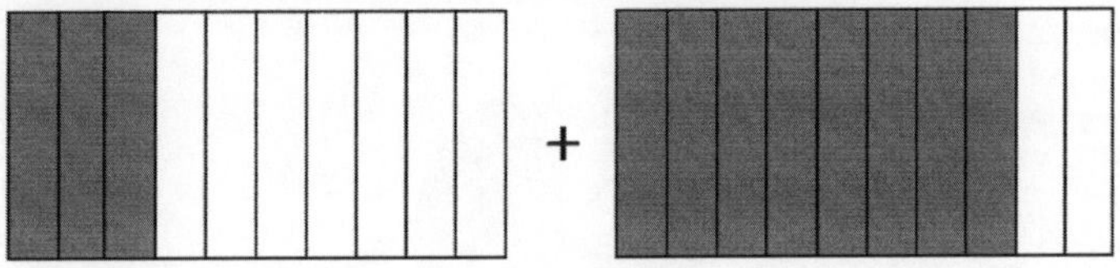

a. 1.08
b. 1.09
c. 1.10
d. 1.11

10. The measure of the angle to the nearest degree is ____. Write your answer in the blank below.

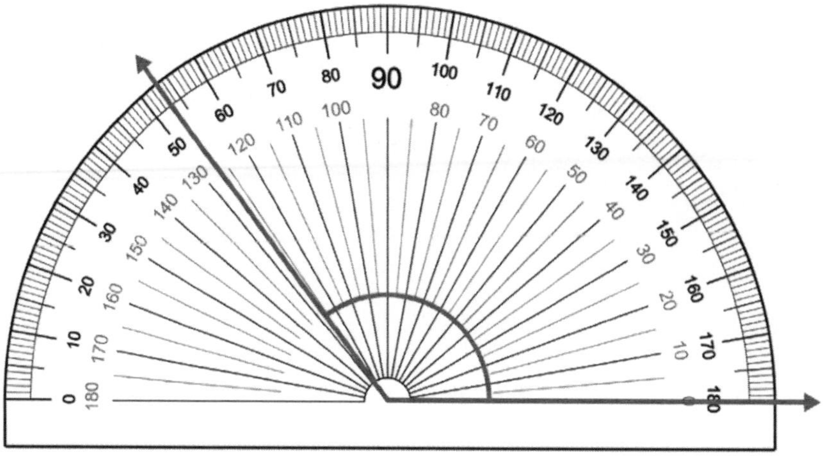

11. All of the equations show correct ways to decompose the fraction except for one. Which choice does NOT belong?

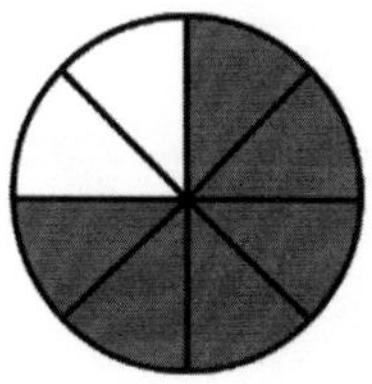

a. $\frac{2}{8}+\frac{2}{8}+\frac{2}{8}=\frac{6}{8}$
b. $\frac{2}{8}+\frac{4}{8}+\frac{1}{8}=\frac{6}{8}$
c. $\frac{3}{8}+\frac{3}{8}=\frac{6}{8}$
d. $\frac{1}{8}+\frac{1}{8}+\frac{1}{8}+\frac{1}{8}+\frac{1}{8}+\frac{1}{8}=\frac{6}{8}$

12. Alex buys 3 gallons of milk each week. How many gallons of milk does he buy in 12 weeks?

a. 18
b. 24
c. 36
d. 48

13. When 751 is rounded to the nearest hundred it becomes ____. Write your answer in the blank below.

14. Isabelle must drive 1,482 miles. She plans to drive approximately the same number of miles per day over the period of 5 days. Which of the following is the best approximation for the number of miles she will drive per day?

a. 250
b. 300
c. 350
d. 400

15. A consultant earned $17,850 over the course of 6 months. Which of the following is the best approximation for the amount of money the consultant earned each month?

a. $2,500
b. $3,000
c. $3,500
d. $4,000

16. Mr. Jacobsen buys 32 boxes of oatmeal. Each box contains 20 packets of oatmeal. How many total packets of oatmeal did he buy? Write your answer in the blank below.

17. Mr. Johnson ordered 1 pizza for every 3 kids in his class. If he ordered 7 pizzas then how many kids does he have in his class? Write your answer in the blank below.

18. If 3 more slices of the circle are shaded in then what fraction would it be?

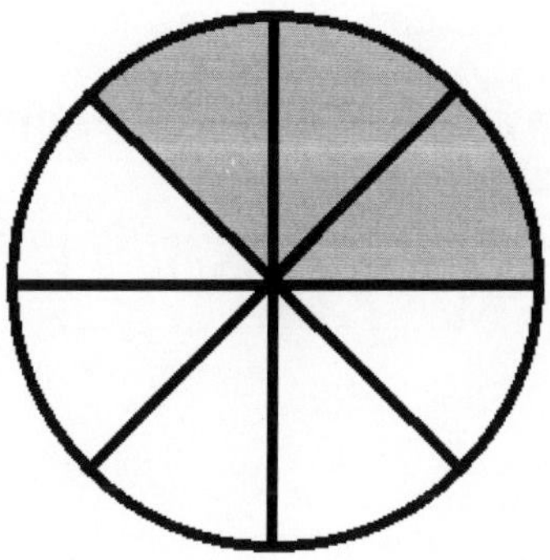

a. $\frac{5}{8}$
b. $\frac{5}{6}$
c. $\frac{2}{3}$
d. $\frac{3}{4}$

19. The number of miles Brad has driven over a period of 3 days is shown in the table below.

Day	Number of Miles
1	275
2	550
3	825

If this pattern continues, how many miles will he have driven after 8 days?

a. 2,000
b. 2,025
c. 2,075
d. 2,200

20. Amber has a large pile of candy. When Amber divides the pile of candy into 5 equal piles, each pile has 31 pieces. How many pieces of candy does Amber have altogether?

a. 145 pieces of candy
b. 146 pieces of candy
c. 151 pieces of candy
d. 155 pieces of candy

21. Jenny will be in a parade and will be throwing out candy. She has 20 pieces of candy, but she thinks that she will need 12 times that much since the parade is so long. How many pieces does she think she needs? Write your answer in the blank below.

22. Morris needs to define an obtuse angle. Which of the following correctly describes the requirements for such an angle?

a. An angle with a measure greater than 180 degrees
b. An angle with a measure greater than 120 degrees
c. An angle with a measure less than 90 degrees
d. An angle with a measure greater than 90 degrees

23. If John works 386 minutes a day, how many minutes does he work in a 5 day work week? Write your answer in the blank below.

24. Which fraction is less than $\frac{12}{20}$?

a. $\frac{24}{40}$
b. $\frac{6}{10}$
c. $\frac{3}{5}$
d. $\frac{1}{5}$

25. Sally eats $\frac{2}{8}$ of a pie, Jesse eats $\frac{1}{8}$ of the same pie, and Lisa eats $\frac{3}{8}$ of the pie. How much of the pie is left?

a. $\frac{1}{4}$
b. $\frac{3}{8}$
c. $\frac{1}{8}$
d. $\frac{1}{2}$

26. Which decimal is equivalent to $\frac{16}{100}$?

a. 0.16
b. 0.61
c. 1.60
d. 16.0

27. An ice cream shop earns $505.75 on Saturday and $815.25 on Sunday. How much money did the shop earn over both days?

a. $1,221
b. $1,321
c. $1,521
d. $1,991

28. Calculate the area of the rectangle below.

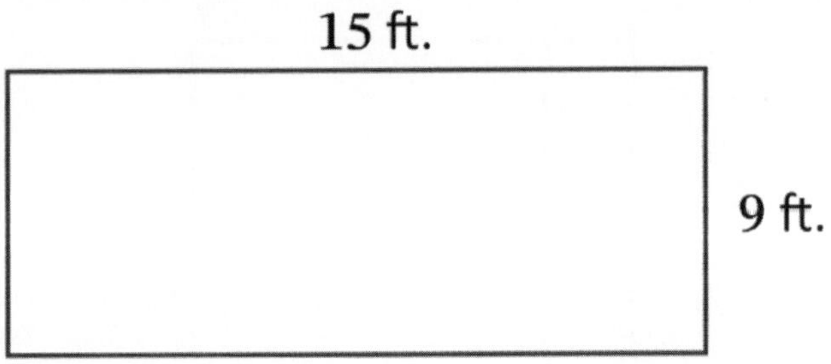

a. 135 square feet
b. 153 square feet
c. 351 square feet
d. 513 square feet

29. A school has 14 classrooms. Each classroom has 22 students in it. How many total students are in the school?

a. 36
b. 288
c. 304
d. 308

30. A teacher took a survey of 4th, 5th, and 6th grade students about their favorite animals.

	Cat	Dog	Fish	Bird
4th Grade	8	10	5	4
5th Grade	10	12	4	4
6th Grade	7	13	2	3

What fraction of 5th grade students chose cats as their favorite animal?

a. $\frac{2}{3}$
b. $\frac{1}{3}$
c. $\frac{12}{30}$
d. $\frac{10}{28}$

31. Blake practices piano 6 days per week for the same amount of time each day. If Blake practices 150 minutes each week, how many minutes does he practice during 2 days?

a. 40 minutes
b. 50 minutes
c. 60 minutes
d. 75 minutes

32. In the rectangle below each small square is one square unit. How many square units make up the area of the entire rectangle?

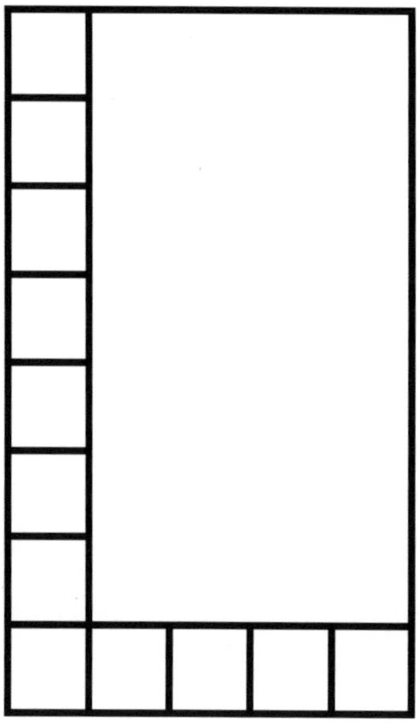

a. 28
b. 40
c. 12
d. 35

33. Hannah weighs approximately 27 pounds. What is her approximate weight, in ounces?

a. 432 ounces
b. 378 ounces
c. 324 ounces
d. 438 ounces

34. Jamal drinks 2 quarts of water per day. How many cups of water does he drink? Write your answer in the blank below.

35. The measure of the angle to the nearest degree is ___. Write your answer in the blank below.

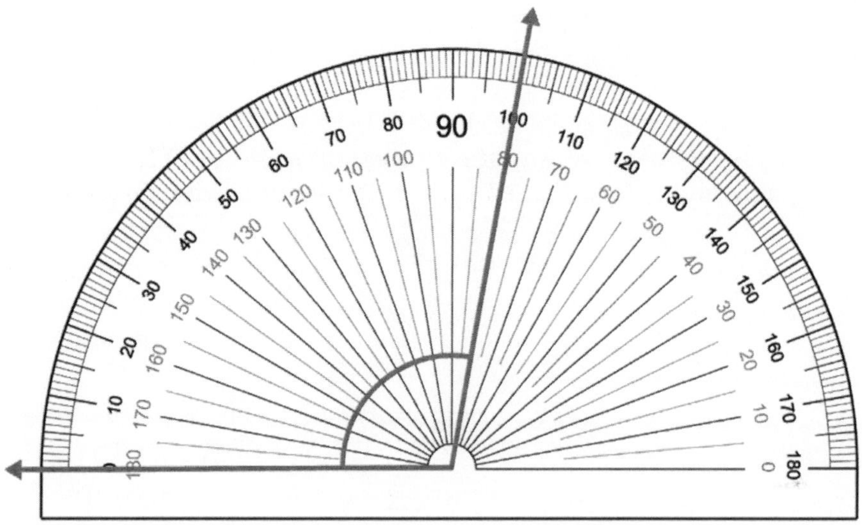

36. Jim drives 1920 miles. He used 6 tanks of gas to drive that far. How many miles can he go on one tank of gas? Write your answer in the blank below.

37. Kay has 180 stickers. She divides the stickers equally among 8 children. Each child receives the same number of stickers. How many extra stickers will be remaining after Kay divides the stickers?

a. 2 stickers
b. 3 stickers
c. 4 stickers
d. 5 stickers

38. The stem and leaf plot shows final exam scores for a statistics class. What is the median score of the students that took the final exam?

Stem	Leaf
5	6
6	7 7 9
7	2 4 7 7 8
8	1 2 2 3 4 8
9	0 2 3 4

Key: 5|6 = 56

a. 81
b. 82
c. 78
d. 67

39. The table shows number of yards and the equivalent number of feet. Sean climbs a rope that is 7 yards long. How many feet did Sean climb? Write your answer in the blank.

Yards	Feet
1	3
2	6
3	9

40. The scores on Mrs. Rodriguez's math test are shown below.

95, 78, 92, 99, 74, 83, 89, 92, 79, 85, 87, 90, 88, 92, 79

Which test score was received by the most students?

a. 78
b. 90
c. 92
d. 79

Answers and Explanations for Test #2

1. C: The first room contains, $6 \times 9 = 54$, chairs. The second contains 32. $54 + 32 = 86$.

2. A: The measure of $\angle ADC$ can be determined by adding the measure of $\angle ADB$ to the measure of $\angle BDC$. $\angle ADB$ is 42° and $\angle BDC$ is 64°, so the sum of these two angles is $42° + 64° = 106°$. The measure of $\angle ADC$ is 106°.

3. B: The fraction, $\frac{8}{12}$, is equivalent to the fraction, $\frac{2}{3}$. The numerator and denominator of the given fraction are both divided by 4 to obtain the model for $\frac{2}{3}$; the fractions are proportional.

4. B: The first diagram represents 1 whole, while the second diagram represents $\frac{2}{5}$. Thus the diagram represents $1\frac{2}{5}$, in its entirety.

5. B: The fraction, $\frac{5}{15}$, is equivalent to the fraction, $\frac{1}{3}$. The numerator and denominator of the given fraction are both divided by 5 to obtain the model for $\frac{1}{3}$; the fractions are proportional.

6. B: $\frac{6}{9}$ can both be reduced to $\frac{2}{3}$. This means they are equivalent.

7. C: The sum of the dollar amounts is equal to $156.78 + $173.35 + $219.65, or $549.78. When adding decimal values, lining up place value is very important.

$$
\begin{array}{r}
{}^{1}1\;{}^{1}5\;{}^{1}6\;.\;{}^{1}7\;8 \\
1\;7\;3\;.\;3\;5 \\
+\;2\;1\;9\;.\;6\;5 \\
\hline
5\;4\;9\;.\;7\;8
\end{array}
$$

8. A: Add 12 minutes to 4:35 P.M. Break apart 12 minutes into 10 minutes + 2 minutes. 4:35 P.M. plus 10 minutes is 4:45 P.M. Now, add 2 more minutes. 4:45 plus 2 minutes is 4:47 P.M. Peter took the cookie tray out of the oven at 4:47 P.M.

9. C: The diagram represents the sum of $\frac{3}{10}$ and $\frac{8}{10}$, or $\frac{11}{10}$, which is equivalent to $1\frac{1}{10}$, or 1.10. The decimals, 0.30 + 0.80, can also be added, which equal 1.10.

10. 127: The right interior row of numbers starts at 0°. Start at 0° and move counterclockwise to meet the other ray. The other ray passes through 127° on the interior row of numbers, so the angle measures 127°.

11. C: The circle represents 1 whole, and the whole is divided into 8 equal shares. 6 out of 8 shares are shaded. $\frac{2}{8} + \frac{4}{8} + \frac{1}{8} = \frac{6}{8}$ does not describe the shaded region because it has a sum of $\frac{7}{8}$, not $\frac{6}{8}$.

12. C: Alex will be 3×12 gallons of milk in 12 weeks, or 36 gallons of milk.

13. 800: Locate the digit in the hundreds place. The number 751 has a 7 in the hundreds place. Now look to the digit to the right. If this digit is 5 or more, round up. If this digit is 4 or less, round down. In this case, the digit to the right of 7 is 5, so 751 rounds up to 800.

14. B: The distance Isabelle drives can be rounded to 1,500 miles; 1,500 miles divided by 5 days is equal to 300 miles driven per day.

15. B: The consultant's earnings can be rounded to \$18,000; \$18,000 divided over 6 months is equal to \$3,000 per month.

16. 640: Each box contains 20 packets, so that's the same as 32×20, which is 640.

17. 21: If 1 pizza feeds 3 people then you can multiply 7 times 3 to figure out that 7 pizzas feeds 21 people.

18. D: If you shaded 3 more of the eighths that would make $\frac{6}{8}$ which reduces to $\frac{3}{4}$.

19. D: Brad drives 275 miles each day. Thus, the total number of miles driven, over a period of days, can be found by adding 275 miles to the number of total miles driven for each previous day. In other words, after 4 days, he drove 1,100 miles. After 5 days, he drove 1,375 miles. After 6 days, he drove 1,650 miles. After 7 days, he drove 1,925 miles. After 8 days, he drove 2,200 miles.

20. D: There are 5 piles of candy, and each pile has 31 pieces. Multiply to find the total number of pieces: $5 \times 31 = 155$. There are 155 pieces of candy altogether.

21. C: The total amount of money donated is \$300 more each additional year. Thus, the total amount donated, over a period of years, can be found by adding 300 dollars to the amount donated for each previous year. In other words, after 6 years, the total amount donated was \$1,750. After 7 years, the total amount donated was \$2,050. After 8 years, the total amount donated was \$2,350. After 9 years, the total amount donated was \$2,650. After 10 years, the total amount donated was \$2,950.

22. D: An obtuse angle has a measure greater than 90 degrees. It may be greater than 120 degrees, but that is not a requirement.

23. 1930: To find the answer multiply 386 times 5.

24. D: The fractions $\frac{24}{40}, \frac{6}{10}$, and $\frac{3}{5}$ are all equivalent to the fraction $\frac{12}{20}$.

$$\frac{12}{20} \times \frac{2}{2} = \frac{24}{40}$$

$$\frac{12}{20} \div \frac{2}{2} = \frac{6}{10}$$

$$\frac{12}{20} \div \frac{4}{4} = \frac{3}{5}$$

So, $\frac{1}{5}$ must be less than $\frac{12}{20}$. Use a common denominator to compare the two fractions. $\frac{1}{5}$ is equivalent to $\frac{4}{20}$. $\frac{4}{20} < \frac{12}{20}$, therefore $\frac{1}{5} < \frac{12}{20}$.

25. A: First add all of the fractions together to find out how much of the pie was eaten. $\frac{2}{8}+\frac{1}{8}+\frac{3}{8}=\frac{6}{8}=\frac{3}{4}$, so that leaves $\frac{1}{4}$ of the pie that was not eaten.

26. A: The fraction $\frac{16}{100}$ represents 16 hundredths. This is equivalent to 1 tenth plus 6 hundredths. This means there will be a 1 in the tenths place and a 6 in the hundredths place. The fraction $\frac{16}{100}$ is equivalent to 0.16.

27. D: Use the standard algorithm to add the two values. Line up the place value and regroup when necessary. Bring the decimal straight down into the answer. $505.75 plus $815.25 equals $1,321.

$$\begin{array}{r} {\scriptstyle 1\,1\ \ 1} \\ 505.75 \\ +815.25 \\ \hline 1321.00 \end{array}$$

28. A: The area of the rectangle is calculated by multiplying the length and the width. The product 15×9 can be calculated using partial products. $10 \times 9 = 90$, and $5 \times 9 = 45$. $90 + 45 = 135$, so the area of the rectangle is 135 square feet.

29. D: To find the answer just multiply 14 times 22.

30. B: There are 10 5th graders that chose cats as their favorite. There are 30 5th graders total. $\frac{10}{30}=\frac{3}{10}$.

31. B: One way to solve this problem is by using a strip diagram. Blake practices 6 days each week, and the total number of minutes each week is 150. 150 split into 6 days is 25.

25	25	25	25	25	25

Each day Blake practices 25 minutes. 2 sessions of 25 minutes can be calculated as 2×25, which is 50. So, 2 sessions is 50 minutes of practice.

32. B: 8 units make up the length and 5 units make up the width. Area is length times width, so $8 \times 5 = 40$.

33. A: There are 16 ounces in one pound. Thus, her approximate weight, in ounces, is equal to the product of 27 and 16; $27 \times 16 = 432$. She weighs approximately 432 ounces.

34. 8. There are 2 cups in 1 pint and 2 pints in 1 quart. There are 4 pints in 2 quarts. Thus, there are 4×2, or 8 cups, in 2 quarts.

35. 100: The left exterior row of numbers starts at 0°. Start at 0° and move clockwise to meet the other ray. The other ray passes through 100° on the exterior row of numbers, so the angle measures 100°.

36. 320: If he uses 6 tanks then 1920 can just be divided by 6 to get 320.

37. C: Each child will receive 22 stickers: $180 \div 8 = 22$ r 4. Since there is a remainder of 4, this means there will be 4 stickers left over.

38. A: The stem and leaf plot shows the tens digit in the stem and the ones digit in the leaf. There are 19 values listed in the stem and leaf plot, so 19 students took the exam. The median score is the value that falls directly in the middle when the numbers are ordered from least to greatest. 81 is the median score since 9 values come before and 9 values come after.

39. 21: There are 3 feet in every yard. The rope is 7 yards long. Multiply the number of yards by 3 to calculate the number of feet. $7 \times 3 = 21$, so Sean climbed 21 feet.

40. C: The score of 92 was received by 3 students, which is more than any other score received; 78 was received by 1 student; 90 was received by 1 student; and 79 was received by 2 students.

How to Overcome Test Anxiety

Just the thought of taking a test is enough to make most people a little nervous. A test is an important event that can have a long-term impact on your future, so it's important to take it seriously and it's natural to feel anxious about performing well. But just because anxiety is normal, that doesn't mean that it's helpful in test taking, or that you should simply accept it as part of your life. Anxiety can have a variety of effects. These effects can be mild, like making you feel slightly nervous, or severe, like blocking your ability to focus or remember even a simple detail.

If you experience test anxiety—whether severe or mild—it's important to know how to beat it. To discover this, first you need to understand what causes test anxiety.

Causes of Test Anxiety

While we often think of anxiety as an uncontrollable emotional state, it can actually be caused by simple, practical things. One of the most common causes of test anxiety is that a person does not feel adequately prepared for their test. This feeling can be the result of many different issues such as poor study habits or lack of organization, but the most common culprit is time management. Starting to study too late, failing to organize your study time to cover all of the material, or being distracted while you study will mean that you're not well prepared for the test. This may lead to cramming the night before, which will cause you to be physically and mentally exhausted for the test. Poor time management also contributes to feelings of stress, fear, and hopelessness as you realize you are not well prepared but don't know what to do about it.

Other times, test anxiety is not related to your preparation for the test but comes from unresolved fear. This may be a past failure on a test, or poor performance on tests in general. It may come from comparing yourself to others who seem to be performing better or from the stress of living up to expectations. Anxiety may be driven by fears of the future—how failure on this test would affect your educational and career goals. These fears are often completely irrational, but they can still negatively impact your test performance.

Elements of Test Anxiety

As mentioned earlier, test anxiety is considered to be an emotional state, but it has physical and mental components as well. Sometimes you may not even realize that you are suffering from test anxiety until you notice the physical symptoms. These can include trembling hands, rapid heartbeat, sweating, nausea, and tense muscles. Extreme anxiety may lead to fainting or vomiting. Obviously, any of these symptoms can have a negative impact on testing. It is important to recognize them as soon as they begin to occur so that you can address the problem before it damages your performance.

The mental components of test anxiety include trouble focusing and inability to remember learned information. During a test, your mind is on high alert, which can help you recall information and stay focused for an extended period of time. However, anxiety interferes with your mind's natural processes, causing you to blank out, even on the questions you know well. The strain of testing during anxiety makes it difficult to stay focused, especially on a test that may take several hours. Extreme anxiety can take a huge mental toll, making it difficult not only to recall test information but even to understand the test questions or pull your thoughts together.

Effects of Test Anxiety

Test anxiety is like a disease—if left untreated, it will get progressively worse. Anxiety leads to poor performance, and this reinforces the feelings of fear and failure, which in turn lead to poor performances on subsequent tests. It can grow from a mild nervousness to a crippling condition. If allowed to progress, test anxiety can have a big impact on your schooling, and consequently on your future.

Test anxiety can spread to other parts of your life. Anxiety on tests can become anxiety in any stressful situation, and blanking on a test can turn into panicking in a job situation. But fortunately, you don't have to let anxiety rule your testing and determine your grades. There are a number of relatively simple steps you can take to move past anxiety and function normally on a test and in the rest of life.

Physical Steps for Beating Test Anxiety

While test anxiety is a serious problem, the good news is that it can be overcome. It doesn't have to control your ability to think and remember information. While it may take time, you can begin taking steps today to beat anxiety.

Just as your first hint that you may be struggling with anxiety comes from the physical symptoms, the first step to treating it is also physical. Rest is crucial for having a clear, strong mind. If you are tired, it is much easier to give in to anxiety. But if you establish good sleep habits, your body and mind will be ready to perform optimally, without the strain of exhaustion. Additionally, sleeping well helps you to retain information better, so you're more likely to recall the answers when you see the test questions.

Getting good sleep means more than going to bed on time. It's important to allow your brain time to relax. Take study breaks from time to time so it doesn't get overworked, and don't study right before bed. Take time to rest your mind before trying to rest your body, or you may find it difficult to fall asleep.

Along with sleep, other aspects of physical health are important in preparing for a test. Good nutrition is vital for good brain function. Sugary foods and drinks may give a burst of energy but this burst is followed by a crash, both physically and emotionally. Instead, fuel your body with protein and vitamin-rich foods.

Also, drink plenty of water. Dehydration can lead to headaches and exhaustion, especially if your brain is already under stress from the rigors of the test. Particularly if your test is a long one, drink water during the breaks. And if possible, take an energy-boosting snack to eat between sections.

Along with sleep and diet, a third important part of physical health is exercise. Maintaining a steady workout schedule is helpful, but even taking 5-minute study breaks to walk can help get your blood pumping faster and clear your head. Exercise also releases endorphins, which contribute to a positive feeling and can help combat test anxiety.

When you nurture your physical health, you are also contributing to your mental health. If your body is healthy, your mind is much more likely to be healthy as well. So take time to rest, nourish your body with healthy food and water, and get moving as much as possible. Taking these physical steps will make you stronger and more able to take the mental steps necessary to overcome test anxiety.

Mental Steps for Beating Test Anxiety

Working on the mental side of test anxiety can be more challenging, but as with the physical side, there are clear steps you can take to overcome it. As mentioned earlier, test anxiety often stems from lack of preparation, so the obvious solution is to prepare for the test. Effective studying may be the most important weapon you have for beating test anxiety, but you can and should employ several other mental tools to combat fear.

First, boost your confidence by reminding yourself of past success—tests or projects that you aced. If you're putting as much effort into preparing for this test as you did for those, there's no reason you should expect to fail here. Work hard to prepare; then trust your preparation.

Second, surround yourself with encouraging people. It can be helpful to find a study group, but be sure that the people you're around will encourage a positive attitude. If you spend time with others who are anxious or cynical, this will only contribute to your own anxiety. Look for others who are motivated to study hard from a desire to succeed, not from a fear of failure.

Third, reward yourself. A test is physically and mentally tiring, even without anxiety, and it can be helpful to have something to look forward to. Plan an activity following the test, regardless of the outcome, such as going to a movie or getting ice cream.

When you are taking the test, if you find yourself beginning to feel anxious, remind yourself that you know the material. Visualize successfully completing the test. Then take a few deep, relaxing breaths and return to it. Work through the questions carefully but with confidence, knowing that you are capable of succeeding.

Developing a healthy mental approach to test taking will also aid in other areas of life. Test anxiety affects more than just the actual test—it can be damaging to your mental health and even contribute to depression. It's important to beat test anxiety before it becomes a problem for more than testing.

Study Strategy

Being prepared for the test is necessary to combat anxiety, but what does being prepared look like? You may study for hours on end and still not feel prepared. What you need is a strategy for test prep. The next few pages outline our recommended steps to help you plan out and conquer the challenge of preparation.

Step 1: Scope Out the Test

Learn everything you can about the format (multiple choice, essay, etc.) and what will be on the test. Gather any study materials, course outlines, or sample exams that may be available. Not only will this help you to prepare, but knowing what to expect can help to alleviate test anxiety.

Step 2: Map Out the Material

Look through the textbook or study guide and make note of how many chapters or sections it has. Then divide these over the time you have. For example, if a book has 15 chapters and you have five days to study, you need to cover three chapters each day. Even better, if you have the time, leave an extra day at the end for overall review after you have gone through the material in depth.

If time is limited, you may need to prioritize the material. Look through it and make note of which sections you think you already have a good grasp on, and which need review. While you are studying, skim quickly through the familiar sections and take more time on the challenging parts.

Write out your plan so you don't get lost as you go. Having a written plan also helps you feel more in control of the study, so anxiety is less likely to arise from feeling overwhelmed at the amount to cover.

Step 3: Gather Your Tools

Decide what study method works best for you. Do you prefer to highlight in the book as you study and then go back over the highlighted portions? Or do you type out notes of the important information? Or is it helpful to make flashcards that you can carry with you? Assemble the pens, index cards, highlighters, post-it notes, and any other materials you may need so you won't be distracted by getting up to find things while you study.

If you're having a hard time retaining the information or organizing your notes, experiment with different methods. For example, try color-coding by subject with colored pens, highlighters, or post-it notes. If you learn better by hearing, try recording yourself reading your notes so you can listen while in the car, working out, or simply sitting at your desk. Ask a friend to quiz you from your flashcards, or try teaching someone the material to solidify it in your mind.

Step 4: Create Your Environment

It's important to avoid distractions while you study. This includes both the obvious distractions like visitors and the subtle distractions like an uncomfortable chair (or a too-comfortable couch that makes you want to fall asleep). Set up the best study environment possible: good lighting and a comfortable work area. If background music helps you focus, you may want to turn it on, but otherwise keep the room quiet. If you are using a computer to take notes, be sure you don't have any other windows open, especially applications like social media, games, or anything else that could distract you. Silence your phone and turn off notifications. Be sure to keep water close by so you stay hydrated while you study (but avoid unhealthy drinks and snacks).

Also, take into account the best time of day to study. Are you freshest first thing in the morning? Try to set aside some time then to work through the material. Is your mind clearer in the afternoon or evening? Schedule your study session then. Another method is to study at the same time of day that you will take the test, so that your brain gets used to working on the material at that time and will be ready to focus at test time.

Step 5: Study!

Once you have done all the study preparation, it's time to settle into the actual studying. Sit down, take a few moments to settle your mind so you can focus, and begin to follow your study plan. Don't give in to distractions or let yourself procrastinate. This is your time to prepare so you'll be ready to fearlessly approach the test. Make the most of the time and stay focused.

Of course, you don't want to burn out. If you study too long you may find that you're not retaining the information very well. Take regular study breaks. For example, taking five minutes out of every hour to walk briskly, breathing deeply and swinging your arms, can help your mind stay fresh.

As you get to the end of each chapter or section, it's a good idea to do a quick review. Remind yourself of what you learned and work on any difficult parts. When you feel that you've mastered the material, move on to the next part. At the end of your study session, briefly skim through your notes again.

But while review is helpful, cramming last minute is NOT. If at all possible, work ahead so that you won't need to fit all your study into the last day. Cramming overloads your brain with more information than it can process and retain, and your tired mind may struggle to recall even previously learned information when it is overwhelmed with last-minute study. Also, the urgent nature of cramming and the stress placed on your brain contribute to anxiety. You'll be more likely to go to the test feeling unprepared and having trouble thinking clearly.

So don't cram, and don't stay up late before the test, even just to review your notes at a leisurely pace. Your brain needs rest more than it needs to go over the information again. In fact, plan to finish your studies by noon or early afternoon the day before the test. Give your brain the rest of the day to relax or focus on other things, and get a good night's sleep. Then you will be fresh for the test and better able to recall what you've studied.

Step 6: Take a Practice Test

Many courses offer sample tests, either online or in the study materials. This is an excellent resource to check whether you have mastered the material, as well as to prepare for the test format and environment.

Check the test format ahead of time: the number of questions, the type (multiple choice, free response, etc.), and the time limit. Then create a plan for working through them. For example, if you have 30 minutes to take a 60-question test, your limit is 30 seconds per question. Spend less time on the questions you know well so that you can take more time on the difficult ones.

If you have time to take several practice tests, take the first one open book, with no time limit. Work through the questions at your own pace and make sure you fully understand them. Gradually work up to taking a test under test conditions: sit at a desk with all study materials put away and set a timer. Pace yourself to make sure you finish the test with time to spare and go back to check your answers if you have time.

After each test, check your answers. On the questions you missed, be sure you understand why you missed them. Did you misread the question (tests can use tricky wording)? Did you forget the information? Or was it something you hadn't learned? Go back and study any shaky areas that the practice tests reveal.

Taking these tests not only helps with your grade, but also aids in combating test anxiety. If you're already used to the test conditions, you're less likely to worry about it, and working through tests until you're scoring well gives you a confidence boost. Go through the practice tests until you feel comfortable, and then you can go into the test knowing that you're ready for it.

Test Tips

On test day, you should be confident, knowing that you've prepared well and are ready to answer the questions. But aside from preparation, there are several test day strategies you can employ to maximize your performance.

First, as stated before, get a good night's sleep the night before the test (and for several nights before that, if possible). Go into the test with a fresh, alert mind rather than staying up late to study.

Try not to change too much about your normal routine on the day of the test. It's important to eat a nutritious breakfast, but if you normally don't eat breakfast at all, consider eating just a protein bar. If you're a coffee drinker, go ahead and have your normal coffee. Just make sure you time it so that the caffeine doesn't wear off right in the middle of your test. Avoid sugary beverages, and drink enough water to stay hydrated but not so much that you need a restroom break 10 minutes into the test. If your test isn't first thing in the morning, consider going for a walk or doing a light workout before the test to get your blood flowing.

Allow yourself enough time to get ready, and leave for the test with plenty of time to spare so you won't have the anxiety of scrambling to arrive in time. Another reason to be early is to select a good seat. It's helpful to sit away from doors and windows, which can be distracting. Find a good seat, get out your supplies, and settle your mind before the test begins.

When the test begins, start by going over the instructions carefully, even if you already know what to expect. Make sure you avoid any careless mistakes by following the directions.

Then begin working through the questions, pacing yourself as you've practiced. If you're not sure on an answer, don't spend too much time on it, and don't let it shake your confidence. Either skip it and come back later, or eliminate as many wrong answers as possible and guess among the remaining ones. Don't dwell on these questions as you continue—put them out of your mind and focus on what lies ahead.

Be sure to read all of the answer choices, even if you're sure the first one is the right answer. Sometimes you'll find a better one if you keep reading. But don't second-guess yourself if you do immediately know the answer. Your gut instinct is usually right. Don't let test anxiety rob you of the information you know.

If you have time at the end of the test (and if the test format allows), go back and review your answers. Be cautious about changing any, since your first instinct tends to be correct, but make sure you didn't misread any of the questions or accidentally mark the wrong answer choice. Look over any you skipped and make an educated guess.

At the end, leave the test feeling confident. You've done your best, so don't waste time worrying about your performance or wishing you could change anything. Instead, celebrate the successful completion of this test. And finally, use this test to learn how to deal with anxiety even better next time.

Review Video: Test Anxiety
Visit mometrix.com/academy and enter code: 100340

Important Qualification

Not all anxiety is created equal. If your test anxiety is causing major issues in your life beyond the classroom or testing center, or if you are experiencing troubling physical symptoms related to your anxiety, it may be a sign of a serious physiological or psychological condition. If this sounds like your situation, we strongly encourage you to seek professional help.

Online Resources

Due to our efforts to try to keep this book to a manageable length, we've created a link that will give you access to all of your online resources:

mometrix.com/resources719/flg4math

It's Your Moment, Let's Celebrate It!

Share your story @mometrixtestpreparation